Liu E

The Travels of Lao Can

Translated by Yang Xianyi and
Gladys Yang

Panda Books

Panda Books

First edition, 1983

Copyright 1983 by CHINESE LITERATURE

ISBN 0-8351-1075-3

Published by CHINESE LITERATURE, Beijing (37), China

Distributed by China Publications Centre (GUOJI SHUDIAN)
P.O. Box 399, Beijing, China

Printed in the People's Republic of China

Preface

THE author of this novel was called Liu E or Liu Tieyun. He was a native of Dantu in Jiangsu, born in 1857. He had one elder brother and three sisters, and his family was one of the earliest to receive western influence. Liu E was a precocious child who received the traditional Chinese literary training, but who also learnt French and mathematics from Catholic priests and wrote books on geometry, trigonometry and medicine. Eccentric as he was brilliant, instead of exerting himself to secure influential friends and pass the official examinations, he took pleasure in scientific studies and made friends with unconventional individuals or vagabonds, having a horror of the smooth-spoken, sycophantic, complacent bureaucracy. For one period when he was a young man he closed his doors even to his friends, shutting himself up to study; but since his family was not wealthy at that time, even if he had possessed a scholar's temperament he could not have continued to study at home in comfort, and therefore he went to Shanghai as a physician; however he was not successful, for he soon turned to business, where he failed again, losing all his capital but gaining considerable experience of human affairs.

In 1888 there was a flood of the Yellow River in Henan and knowing that the officials responsible were entirely ignorant of river engineering, he offered his services to Minister Wu Hengqian, who was much impressed by him. Thereupon Liu E directed and shared the work of the labourers, undertaking all the difficult tasks from which his colleagues shrank; and thus when the work was successfully completed his reputation was established. As a reward for his services Wu Hengqian promoted him, but he gave his official title to his brother, preferring to remain a private citizen, and devoted himself next to the work of making a map of the Yellow River. Scarcely was this task finished when there was another flood of the river in Shandong, and Provincial Governor Zhang Yao asked him to be one of his advisers. Zhang Yao had numerous advisers on river conservancy, but none of them had any practical knowledge of the subject. The consensus of opinion was that the river banks should be widened, the chief exponent of this theory being a certain Shi Shanchang; but Liu E strongly opposed this method, and wrote seven memoranda urging that the river should be deepened instead of widened.

In 1894, upon the outbreak of the Sino-Japanese war, he returned to the south. The Chinese army was then massed at the northern frontier, but he pointed out the possibility that the Japanese might be making a feint at attacking the north-eastern provinces in order to launch a surprise attack against China's chief naval harbour and destroy the Chinese fleet. His warning fell upon deaf ears, but events proved him to have been correct.

Shortly after he was given an official title, and spent two years in the capital urging the government to build railways and develop industry in order to strengthen and enrich the country. Thus he advocated the building of a railway between Tianjin and Zhenjiang, but without success. He then turned his energies to promoting a scheme for opening an iron-mine in Shanxi, and in this he was successful, although this project was responsible for much of his subsequent unpopularity. On account of the poverty of the country he believed it would be wise to invite westerners to invest in the mine; but the contract stipulated that after thirty years the ownership of the mine should revert to China. Unfortunately the terms of the contract were later not strictly observed, and Liu E's motives were misunderstood or deliberately misinterpreted by his enemies, who declared that he was a traitor working in the pay of foreign devils.

It was in fact true that by this time Liu E was a very rich man, but no evidence has been brought forward to prove that his wealth was gained in any dishonest way, and his prosperity was probably due simply to a shrewd business sense. When he knew, for instance, that the Tianjin-Pukou Railway was to be built, he realised that Pukou, near Nanjing, would become prosperous, and he bought over a thousand Chinese acres of property there, of which he later presented four hundred acres to the government as the site for the railway. His wealth enabled him to indulge his passion for curios, and he had houses in Beijing, Suzhou, Shanghai, Huaian and Nanjing, the latter containing one room built entirely of bricks and tiles of the Han dynasty. At the time of the Yi He Tuan Uprising,* when anti-foreign feeling was most intense, he was living in great luxury in the International Concession in Shanghai, openly and osten-

* The Boxer Uprising.

tatiously entertaining foreign friends. When the foreign army entered Beijing and the Empress Dowager fled, the citizens of the capital were in danger of starving although the Imperial Granary was filled with grain. Russian troops had seized the Imperial Granary, but they had no use for rice, and Liu E went to Beijing and bought all the rice in the granary very cheaply, to distribute it among the people. He was later impeached on the charge of selling government rice without permission, but he escaped arrest in the International Concession in Shanghai.

Early in the twentieth century, Shang-dynasty oracle bones were discovered in excavations at Anyang in Henan, and Liu E was the first man to realise their significance for the study of ancient Chinese history. In the autumn of 1902 he bought great quantities of these bones in Beijing, and later brought them to the attention of his friend Luo Zhenyu, who became the first authority on the subject.

During these years China's sovereignty was increasingly menaced, but the government was too effete to counter the danger, and voices raised in warning or to advocate reforms were simply cries in the wilderness. Unable to take an active part in any constructive programme, in 1905 Liu E wrote *The Travels of Lao Can*. Three years later he went south, and in the summer of 1908 was exiled to Xinjiang, then a region as desolate and remote as the Siberia of Imperial Russia. His presumption in distributing rice to the Beijing refugees during the Yi He Tuan Uprising might have been forgiven him, but the Chinese were increasingly resentful of the encroachments of foreigners upon their rights, and the iron-mine opened at Liu E's instigation was a constant source of irritation to his compatriots. Thus he was impeached, his property and many of his curios were confiscated, and he himself died of paralysis in Urumchi in 1909.

In his life-time Liu E had achieved not a little. His work on the Yellow River, the opening of the Shanxi iron-mine, the distribution of rice to starving people in Beijing, the discovery of the oracle bones and the writing of *The Travels of Lao Can* were achievements any single one of which might have made a man proud. But active, creative and at times even luxurious as was his life, it was tinged throughout with bitterness and melancholy, the melancholy of all far-sighted Chinese of that period, who, while they might lead the life of cultured epicureans themselves, could not fail to realise that their traditional society with all that they valued was passing away, and the future offered no hope. Thus his book was an expression of a deep pessimism, for he knew that all his efforts could only serve to patch up something that was beyond repair. In his own introduction to *The Travels of Lao Can* he explained that the book was wrung from him as a cry of anguish: "Now we grieve for our own life, for our country, for our society and for our culture. The greater our grief the more bitter our outcry; and thus this book was written. The game of chess is drawing to a close and we are growing old. How can we refrain from lamentation?" So he expressed his sadness at the decadence of the Qing dynasty.

This novel is largely autobiographical, for the hero is easily recognisable as Liu E by his profession of physician, his interest in the Yellow River and his attitude towards officialdom in general. The first chapter

of the book is allegorical. Huang Ruihe (the character
"huang" meaning yellow in Chinese) symbolises the
Yellow River, whose sickness broke out every year and
could not be cured by ordinary physicians. The boat
in danger of being wrecked is China, the four men at
the helm being the four ministers of war, the six old
masts standing for the six old departments of war and
two new masts for the two newly created departments.
The length of the boat was two hundred and forty feet,
symbolising the twenty-four provinces of China, while
the thirty feet on the north-east side were the three provinces of the north-east, and the ten feet on the east stood
for Shandong Province. China in the past had relied
upon experience and precedent in guiding the ship of
state, but such methods would not serve in time of crisis,
and the gift of a compass to the pilot symbolises the
scientific spirit of the West which would enable states-
men to set a definite course and take effective steps to
follow it. The description of those who instigated
trouble and advocated a resort to violence suggests that
the writer was against revolution.

Of the other characters in the novel, Yu Xian was
drawn from life, being the leader of the Yi He Tuan
Uprising who won fame as an official in Shandong;
while Zhang Yao, the governor of Shandong, is the
Governor Zhang of the novel, and Shi Shanchang, Liu
E's chief antagonist in river conservancy, is probably
the Inspector Shi of the book.

Unfortunately, the novel was never completed, and
many people believe that certain parts of it were not
written by Liu E himself. Chapters Nine, Ten and
Eleven which are omitted from this translation are said
by the author's grandson to have been altered by the

editor when the book was first published in instalments in a Tianjin newspaper. These chapters deal mainly with a prophecy of coming events, later partially fulfilled; but since they almost certainly contain interpolations, and their tone is at variance with that of the rest of the book, we have not included them in this translation. We have also omitted Chapters Sixteen, Eighteen and Nineteen and part of Chapter Twenty because they concern a murder story in which there is a large supernatural element, again quite alien to the realism of the first part of the book. At least one preface to the novel states that this part of the book was written by the author's son and inserted as an interlude. Chinese novels are as a rule so discursive and loosely constructed that condensation does not necessarily harm them, and such omissions as we have made we feel justified in making, on the grounds that the authorship is doubtful, the subject matter is of comparatively little interest, and the omissions do not detract from the development of the story, which, as previously stated, was never brought to a conclusion.

By describing what Lao Can sees and hears on his travels, the author fiercely attacked the injustices he witnessed and exposed the so-called "honest and upright officials" as hypocrites who tried to rise to power at the expense of the people. This, objectively, helped readers to realise that they could never place any hope in the ruling bureaucrats and thus shows the author's sympathy for the poor. However, Liu E supported feudalism and opposed the bourgeois democratic revolution and Yi He Tuan's struggles against imperialist aggression. This shows the limitations of his age and class.

The Travels of Lao Can has been circulating for fifty years and many people think highly of Liu E's mastery of language. The use of language, observations and detailed descriptions all show the author's originality. Among late Qing-dynasty novels, *The Travels of Lao Can* is, artistically, a prominent work.

Yang Xianyi

Chapter One

IT is said that outside the East Gate of Dengzhou City
in Shandong there is a great mountain called Penglai
and on the mountain there is a pavilion called the Penglai Pavilion. This pavilion stands with painted roofs
and pearly screens amidst clouds and rain, surpassingly
magnificent. On the west it overlooks the city with
its myriad inhabitants wrapped in mist, and on the east
it overlooks the ocean with its tumbling waves stretching
for a thousand miles. So in the afternoon the city
people often bring wine and food here and spend the
night in the pavilion, in order to watch the sun rise
over the sea the next day at dawn. This is an old established custom; but of this no more.

Our story is concerned with the year that a traveller
came here whose name was Lao Can. His family
name actually was Tie and his personal name Ying, but
he had taken the pen-name "Patcher of the Derelict"
after the monk "Lazy and Derelict" of the Tang dynasty, whose name is associated with baked potatoes. Since
everybody liked and respected him, they just called
him Lao Can (Mr. Derelict), and, without anyone knowing how it came about, Lao Can became his other
name. He was little more than thirty years old and
had been born south of the Yangzi River. He had studied some poetry and history, but since he did not know
how to write examination essays he could not pass the

examinations, so no one would invite him to teach; and as for a trade, he felt he was too old to learn any, and doomed to failure if he tried. Actually his father was an official of the third or fourth rank, but because he was strait-laced and did not know how to grasp money, when he returned home after holding office for twenty years he had to pawn his clothes to pay his travelling expenses. It was obvious then that he had no money for his son.

Now since Lao Can had no family portion and no profession to follow, naturally cold and hunger gradually overtook him. He was already in a desperate plight when heaven took pity on him, and a Taoist priest arrived with a clapper, saying that he had been taught by skilled men their divine art, and could cure all diseases; and indeed when people on the street asked him to cure them, they were always healed. Lao Can therefore asked him to be his tutor, and learned some of his prescriptions, after which he wandered with clapper in hand to make a living by curing people's diseases.

He wandered some twenty years over the length and breadth of China, and this year he had just come to a place in Shandong called Qiancheng, where there was a rich man named Huang Ruihe who had a curious disease, for his body was covered with boils, so that every year there would always be a few holes perforated. Some might be cured one year, but the next year more holes would appear in some other part of the body, and although many years had passed, nobody could cure this disease; but it always broke out in summer and by late autumn was better again. In spring that year when Lao Can passed this place, Mr. Huang's steward asked him if he could cure this sickness. "There is a way," he replied, "but you may not listen to me. I will try my small skill, and if you wish to put an end to this sickness it should not be difficult, for all you have to do is follow an ancient prescription which is infallible. For all other diseases there are prescriptions left by the Yellow Emperor, but for this disease there is a prescription left by Yu, the Pacifier of the Flood. Later, in the Tang dynasty, a certain Wang Jing came into possession of this prescription, but after him nobody knew it. Today by great good fortune I know the prescription too."

Thereupon Mr. Huang kept Lao Can to cure his illness, and, strange to relate, whereas in the past after one place was cured another would become perforated, this year although there were small boils, not a single hole appeared. Thus Mr. Huang was overjoyed, and presently mid-autumn passed, when the danger period was over. Everybody felt that since Mr. Huang had suffered from these perforations for more than ten years, this was a great event, and they were all exceedingly happy; so they engaged a repertory company and performed plays for three days to thank the gods. They also made a pyramid of chrysanthemum flowers in the western sitting-room, and feasted every day, enjoying themselves to their hearts' content.

One day when Lao Can had finished his lunch, because he had drunk a cup too many he felt drowsy and went to his room to lie down on a sofa and rest. No sooner had he closed his eyes, however, than two men came in, one of whom was called Learning and the other Intelligence. These were his two best friends, and they said together, "What are you doing at home on such a fine day?"

Lao Can hastily rose to his feet and asked them to sit down, saying, "These days I have had too much food and wine, and I feel rather disgruntled."

"We are just off to Dengzhou District to visit the Penglai Pavilion," said the two men, "and we came specially to invite you. We have already hired a cart for you, so pack up your baggage quickly and we will start."

Lao Can's baggage was not very bulky, consisting only of a few books and some scientific instruments, so it was easy to pack, and they were soon seated in their carts. Then passing wind and dew it was not long before they reached Dengzhou, where they found two guest rooms under the pavilion in which they stayed to enjoy the mirage at sea. The next day Lao Can remarked, "Everybody says the sunrise is a beautiful sight. Du Fu says in one poem, 'The sun rises like a ball tossed up by the ocean.' Why shouldn't we stay awake tonight to see the sunrise?"

"If you feel like it," replied the others, "we will certainly keep you company."

Although in autumn night and day are of equal length, still after sunset and before sunrise the light is reflected by the atmosphere so that it seems as if the night were shorter. The three men opened two bottles of wine, brought out the food they had with them, and feasted and talked until gradually the east had grown quite bright. Actually it was still some time before sunrise, and this brightness was caused by light reflected by the atmosphere. The three men talked a little longer, and then Intelligence said, "It is nearly time now; why not go up to the pavilion to wait for it?"

"You can hear how strong the wind is," said Learning, "and there are big windows on top, so that it will be colder there than in this room. We had better put on more clothes."

Each did as he suggested. Taking their telescopes and carrying rugs they climbed the winding staircase at the back of the pavilion. When they reached the pavilion they sat down at a table by the window and looked towards the east; but all they could see were white waves like hills in the sea stretching without end, while in the north-east were several islands like wisps of smoke: the nearest was called Long Mountain Island and the further ones Great Bamboo and Great Black. By the pavilion the wind shrieked as if it would shake the building. Clouds towered one above the other in the sky, and one great cloud from the north flew to the centre and pressed down upon the rest, crushing a cloud in the east harder and harder, neither giving way to the other, but forming fantastic shapes. After some time the clouds were suffused with red, and Intelligence said, "Well, Lao Can, judging by this light, we shan't see the sunrise today."

"The wind and the waves are enough for me," replied Lao Can, "so that even if I don't see the sun I shall not consider the trip in vain."

Learning, who was gazing through his telescope, said, "Look westwards where there is a black thread rising and sinking with the waves; it must be a steamboat passing."

Thereupon the other two took out their telescopes and focussed on that point, and presently they said, "Yes, yes. See, there is a very thin black thread on the horizon, which must be a boat." They watched it for a little while and then the steamboat passed.

Intelligence was still holding his telescope and scanning all sides very attentively, when suddenly he exclaimed, "Oh! Look at that junk in great danger out there among the huge waves."

"Where?" asked the others.

"Look north-east," said Intelligence, "where the white foam appears. Isn't that Long Mountain Island? It is on this side of the island, gradually drawing near."

The other two looked through their telescopes and cried, "Ah, it certainly is in great danger! Fortunately it is coming this way, and it is less than ten miles from the shore."

After nearly an hour had passed the boat had drawn fairly near. The three men watched it attentively through their telescopes and saw that it was about two hundred and forty feet long and of considerable size. The captain was sitting on the bridge, and four men under him were looking after the helm. Fore and aft there were six old masts with six old sails and two masts with one new sail and one that was slightly worn, making eight masts in all. The boat was heavily laden and must have had all manner of merchandise in its hold. There were many passengers on the deck, both men and women, but there were no awnings to protect them from the sun and wind, just as in the third-class carriages of the Tianjin-Beijing trains. Their faces were buffeted by the north wind and their bodies drenched with spray, as they sat there, wet, cold, hungry and frightened: all the people on the boat seemed to be in a desperate state. Under the sails there were two men to each sail in charge of the riggings, and there were many people in the bow and on deck dressed like sailors.

Although the boat was two hundred and forty feet long, it was damaged in many places. One part about thirty feet long on the north-east side was already broken through, letting the water pour in, while another part, about ten feet long on the east side, was letting water in too; and there was no part that was not battered. The eight men at the sails really had their heart in their work, but each worked at his own task as if they were on eight different boats, so that there was no co-operation between them. As for the sailors, they did nothing but run about among the men and women passengers on board, and at first it was not clear what they were doing; but when the three friends watched them carefully through their telescopes they saw that they were robbing the passengers of their rations and stripping them of their clothes.

When Learning saw this clearly, he could not help exclaiming, "Those damned scoundrels! See, the boat may sink at any moment, and yet instead of trying to save it and bring it quickly to the shore they are maltreating innocent people. It makes me furious."

"There is no need to worry," said Intelligence, "for the boat is now only two or three miles away, and when it reaches the coast we can go on board to remonstrate with them."

Just as he was speaking, however, they suddenly saw some people on the boat being killed and thrown into the sea, and at the same time the course was changed and the boat headed east again. Learning, stamping with rage, fumed, "So many innocent lives on board — isn't it a pity that they should perish at the hands of a few sailors?" Then after a moment's reflection he added, "But fortunately there happen to be a number of fishing boats at the foot of the mountain. Why shouldn't we jump into one and go there to kill those sailors and replace them by others, so saving the lives of the people on board? That would be a good deed and give us great satisfaction."

"Although this plan is good," said Intelligence, "it is rather rash, and may be impracticable. What do you think, Lao Can?"

Lao Can laughed. "It is a very wonderful plan," he said to Learning, "only I would like to know how many regiments you are going to take with you?"

"How can you be so flippant?" said Learning angrily. "Those people are desperate. We must save them at once. Of course we three must go. Where can we find so many regiments of men?"

"In that case," rejoined Lao Can, "since there are over two hundred sailors on the boat, if we three want to kill them, I am afraid we shall be killed ourselves and will never succeed. What do you think?"

After a little thought Learning decided that he was right, so he said, "Then what would you do? Would you just watch them being killed?"

"I do not think the people in charge of the boat are necessarily wicked," replied Lao Can, "but there are two reasons why the situation has become so desperate. Firstly, those people on the Pacific can only live in a pacific manner; when the sea is calm they can guide their boat with ease, but their nature is such that when they encounter storms they become demoralised. They were not prepared to meet a storm today so they have all been thrown into the greatest confusion. Secondly, they do not possess a compass, for ordinarily when the weather is fine they follow the old tradition and steer by the stars in the sky, without making serious mistakes regarding their direction; this is what we call 'depending upon heaven for existence'. But now they have run into this bad weather when the sun and stars are hidden by clouds, so they have nothing to rely upon. It is not that they don't want to do well, only they do not know the direction, and so the further they go the more mistakes they make. The best plan now would be to follow Learning's suggestion and take a fishing boat to catch them up; for since their boat is heavy and ours is light we shall certainly overtake them, and once we have overtaken them we can give them a compass so that they will know the direction and be able to set their course. Then we should also tell the captain the difference in the art of navigation during storms. Once they listen to us there is no reason why they shouldn't reach the coast directly."

"What Lao Can says is quite right," said Intelligence, "and we had better go about it quickly. Otherwise the people in that boat are certainly doomed."

As they were speaking the three descended from the pavilion and ordered their servants to look after the baggage. Then, empty-handed but for their most accurate compass, measuring instruments and the other instruments necessary for navigation, they went down to the harbour at the foot of the mountain where the fishing boats were moored. They chose a swift boat, hoisted the sail and headed out to sea. Luckily there was a north wind, so whether they went east or west they had the wind at their side to facilitate sailing.

Presently they drew near to the big boat which they were still keeping under close observation through their telescopes. When they were about thirty yards away they could hear the words spoken on board, and it seemed that, besides the sailors who were robbing the passengers, there were also some other people making fine speeches, whom they heard saying, "You people have all paid for your passage; moreover this boat is the public property left by your ancestors. Now those in charge have allowed it to lapse into a most deplorable condition, so that the lives of all of you, old and young alike, are jeopardised. Are you going to sit there quietly waiting for death? If you cannot find some way to save yourselves, you are indeed slaves."

Most of the passengers whom they upbraided were dumbfounded, but some amongst them came forward and said, "You have just put into words the woes of our hearts which we could not express. Now that you have enlightened us we are indeed very grateful, only may we ask what we should do?"

"You know that in this world nothing can be done without money," answered the speakers. "Let each of you contribute some money; then we shall exert all our strength and summon up all our resolution, relying on a few men to shed their blood to secure our safety forever. Would not this be well?" All the passengers clapped their hands in approval.

When Learning heard this from a distance, he said to the two others, "I didn't know there were such heroes on board. If we had known earlier we need not have come."

"In that case let us furl a few sails and follow their boat slowly to watch what they will do," said Intelligence. "If they are really capable then we can turn back."

"You are quite right," said Lao Can. "It seems to me that these people may not really be men of action, only making use of some modern catchwords to cheat people of their money."

Then the three lowered their sails and followed the big boat slowly until they saw the passengers collect a sum of money and give it to the speakers to see what they would do. However those orators, after collecting the money, chose a place where the people could not reach them, and entrenching themselves there shouted aloud, "You cold-blooded reptiles, why don't you go at once and beat the men at the helm?" And again, "Why don't you kill all the people in charge of the boat?" There were then some foolish young men who followed their advice, some going to beat the men at the helm, others going to curse the captain of the boat; but they were all killed or thrown into the sea.

The orators then cried aloud from a high place, "Why don't you organise yourselves? If all the people on the boat work together you will certainly be a match for them."

However, there were also some old and prudent people on the boat, who called out, "Don't do anything rash. If you act in such a way, then before the battle is won you will have sunk the boat. You must on no account do that."

Intelligence, hearing this, said to Learning, "So the heroes here only collect money for themselves, calling upon others to shed blood."

"Lucky that a few people had some sense," said Lao Can, "otherwise the boat would have sunk even sooner."

Even as they were speaking, they hoisted their sails and soon drew abreast of the big boat. The sailor with the grappling iron grappled the big boat, and the three jumped on board. They went to the helm, bowed, took out their compass and measuring instruments and presented them. The men at the helm received them courteously and asked them how these instruments should be used and what advantages they had. They were in the middle of a discussion when an uproar arose on the lower deck, and some sailors cried, "Captain! Captain! You really must not be deceived by these men. They are using a foreign compass, so they must be traitors sent here by foreign devils; that is how they possess this compass. You had better quickly have them put in chains and killed in order to avoid future trouble; for if you talk to them any more, or use their compass, you will be considered as having accepted the money of foreign devils, and then they will come and take over the boat."

All the passengers were swayed by this uproar, so that even those heroes who made speeches started shouting, "These are traitors who want to sell our boat. Kill them! Kill them!" The captain and the men at the helm were in a quandary when one among them, who was the uncle of the captain, said, "Gentlemen, you came with the best intentions, but you can do nothing in face of the angry mob. You'd better go quickly." And so, shedding tears, they went back to the small boat. But the people on the big boat were not yet placated, and when they saw them board the small boat they seized the planks broken by the waves and hurled them at the small boat. It was impossible for such a small fishing boat to stand up to several hundred people bombarding it with all their strength, and in a little while it was broken to pieces and sank into the sea. If you want to know what happened to the three men, you must read the next chapter.

Chapter Two

IT is said that when Lao Can was on the fishing boat he was attacked by people and sank into the sea, and, knowing that he could not escape death, he closed his eyes and resigned himself to his fate. He felt like a falling leaf, floating and fluttering, and soon he sank to the bottom of the sea. Then he heard someone shouting in his ear: "Sir, you had better get up now. The meal has been ready in the dining-hall for a long time."

Lao Can hurriedly opened his eyes and said in bewilderment, "Oh, so it was only a dream."

When another few days had passed Lao Can said to Mr. Huang's steward, "Now the weather is becoming cold, your master's sickness will not grow worse again. Next year if you need me I shall be glad to offer my services, but now I want to go to Jinan to see the scenery of the Daming Lake." The steward could not keep him, so he prepared a farewell feast for him that evening, put a thousand taels of silver in a parcel and presented them to him as his fee; then Lao Can thanked him, packed his baggage, said good-bye and went away by cart. Along the road he saw red leaves on the autumn hills and yellow chrysanthemums in old gardens, so that he was not bored.

When he reached Jinan and entered the city, there were flowing streams by every house and willow trees by every door, which delighted him even more than the scenery of the south. He went to Commissioner's Road and found a hotel called High Promotion. Here he deposited his baggage, paid for the cart and tipped the driver, ate some dinner and went to sleep. The next morning when he had got up and had some breakfast, he walked the streets sounding his clapper and pursuing his profession. After lunch he walked to the Sparrow-flower Bridge where he hired a small boat and paddled along towards the north. Soon he reached the Lixia Pavilion, so he stepped ashore and went in, and when he entered the gate he saw a pavilion, the paint of which was practically all worn away, and on it were hanging two scrolls on which was written:

> "The pavilion is as ancient as history;
> Many are the scholars of Jinan."

This couplet was written by Du Fu and copied by a man called He Shaoji. Although there were a few houses by the pavilion they held no interest for him, so he returned to the boat and went westwards, and soon he reached the temple of Tiexuan, the man at the beginning of the Ming dynasty who denounced Prince Yan as a usurper of the throne. Later generations admired his loyalty, and so in spring and autumn the local people often made sacrifice to him.

When he reached the temple he looked southwards and saw on the other side of the lake the Mount of a Thousand Buddhas. There were temples and monasteries, some high and some low, scattered among the grey pines and green cypresses: the red were red as fire, the white as white as snow, the blue as blue as indigo and the green as green as emerald, while here and there were a few red maples. It looked like a big painting by Zhao Qianli, the Song-dynasty painter, only made into a screen a dozen miles long. Lao Can was delighting in the scene when suddenly he heard the chant of a fisherman, and when he looked down he saw the lake as clear as a mirror. The inverted image of the mountain was reflected with great distinctness in the lake, and the pavilions and trees upon it looked exceptionally bright, so that it seemed even more beautiful and clear than the real mountain above. Ascending the south bank of the lake one came to the city again, but the sight was screened by reeds. It was blossom time and a canopy of white flowers in the setting sun, with the mist rising from the water, seemed like a pink carpet strewn as cushions between the two hills, presenting a most curious spectacle.

"Since the scenery is so beautiful," thought Lao Can, "how is it there are no people here enjoying themselves?" He looked for a while then turned back and saw on the pillars inside the great gate a couple of scrolls on which was written:

> "Lotus on four sides, willows on three,
> Mountains within the city and lakes over half the city."

He nodded and said to himself, "That is true." Then he went in and saw this was the sacrificial hall for Tiexuan, and in the east there was a lotus pool encircled by winding corridors, on the east side of which was a moon-gate, and east of the moon-gate were three old chambers bearing the inscription: "This is the ancient temple of Water Nymph." There were also a couple of old scrolls inside the temple on which was written:

> "One cup of cold water with autumn chrysanthe-
> mums;
> At midnight the painted barge pierces through the
> lotus."

After visiting the temple he returned by boat to the back
of the pavilion, where lotus leaves and flowers pressed
upon both sides of the boat. The leaves were withered
and rustled as they brushed against the boat, while water
birds, startled by his paddle, flew away crying. Old
lotus seeds drifted continuously into the cabin, and as
Lao Can picked up two and ate them, the boat reached
the bridge.

Lao Can had no sooner reached the bridge than he
saw crowds of people, some carrying goods to sell, some
pushing little carts, some seated in blue sedan-chairs carried by two bearers. He noticed behind one sedan-chair
a runner wearing a red-tasselled hat, with a folder
under his arm, posting along as if his life depended on
it, wiping his sweat with his handkerchief as he ran
with lowered head. There were children of five or six
on the street who did not know how to get out of the
way, and the chair-bearer knocked one down, who
started crying. The child's mother hastily came up and
asked, "Who knocked you down? Who knocked you
down?" She asked twice, but the child simply cried and
said nothing, and only after she had repeated the question several times did the child answer, crying, "The
man carrying the chair." When the woman looked up
the chair was already over half a mile away, so she
could do nothing but take the child back, grumbling
and scolding.

As Lao Can went southwards from the bridge and

walked slowly towards his street, he happened to raise his head and see a white paper, about one foot by seven or eight inches, pasted on the wall. In the middle was written "Drum Stories", and at the side in small characters "At the Lake Pavilion on the twenty-fourth". The ink was not yet dry and the notice had evidently just been pasted up, but he did not know what it was about, not having seen such advertisements in other places before. He walked along thinking as he went. Then he heard two pedlars saying, "Tomorrow White Sister is going to tell stories. We had better stop our business and go to hear her." When he came to the street he also heard someone in a shop say, "Last time White Sister told stories you asked for leave. Tomorrow it will be my turn." Everywhere he passed this seemed to form the general topic of conversation, and he marvelled to himself, saying, "Who can this White Sister be, and what kind of stories does she tell? How is it that with only one advertisement the whole city seems to be in an uproar?" Walking on he soon reached his hotel, and when he went in the waiter came and asked, "What will you have for supper?"

When Lao Can had given his order he asked casually, "What is the Drum Story? How is it so many people are interested?"

"Don't you know, sir?" said the waiter. "The Drum Story is the local music of Shandong. One drum and a pair of castanets are used, so it is called 'The Castanet-drum', and some old stories are told. It was really nothing to talk about until the two sisters — White Sister and Black Sister — appeared in the Wang family. White Sister, whose name is Little Jade, was a prodigy, and when she was only twelve or thirteen she learned the art of telling stories. But she felt that the country tunes were uninteresting, so she went to the theatres to study and learnt all the opera tunes; and the songs of all the famous actors she learnt after only one hearing. Because she has a good voice she can sing as high as she likes, and because her breath control is good she can sustain a note as long as she pleases. Moreover she also learnt all the southern tunes and incorporated them into the Drum Story music, and so in two or three years she developed this new music. The result is that whoever hears her singing, no matter where he comes from or what his rank in society, is bound to feel moved. Now there is an advertisement announcing a performance tomorrow. If you don't believe me you can go tomorrow and then you will see for yourself. Only if you want to hear it you will have to go early, for although the performance begins at one o'clock in the afternoon, if you go there at ten o'clock there will be no seats."

However even after hearing this Lao Can still felt somewhat sceptical.

The next morning he got up at six o'clock and went first to the South Gate to see Shun's Well; then he went outside the gate to the foot of the mountain to see the place where in ancient times Shun was supposed to have ploughed. When he returned to the hotel it was already nine o'clock, and after a quick breakfast he went to the theatre, arriving there at about ten o'clock. This Lake Pavilion was a large theatre with over a hundred tables before the stage, but when he went in there was already a full house, with only seven or eight tables left, all marked "Reserved" for the inspector, the examiner, the governor and other high officials. Lao Can looked round for a long time but could not find a place, so he took two hundred cash from his sleeve and gave them to an attendant, who then fetched him a small stool so that he could sit down among the others. He saw a table on the stage on which there was a drum, and on the drum were two pieces of iron which he knew must be the castanets; by the side was a three-stringed guitar, and behind the table there were two chairs. There was no one on the stage, and he felt rather amused to see such a large stage entirely empty. Some twenty or thirty vendors, carrying baskets on their heads, were selling refreshments in the theatre for those who had come without their lunch.

At about eleven o'clock more sedan-chairs and carriages came to the door, all belonging to officials who were wearing ordinary dress and had brought their servants. By twelve o'clock all the reserved tables in front were full, but people continued to come in, and the attendants brought small stools for them and squeezed them in among the others. The newcomers greeted each other, some of them kneeling on one knee and some giving a more casual greeting, but most of them knelt on one knee. They all talked at the top of their voices, laughing and chattering. The other tables were occupied by people who looked like merchants or local scholars, all gossiping noisily. Because there were so many people it was impossible to catch what they were saying, and he did not try.

When it was about half past twelve a man came out from behind the screen wearing a blue cloth gown; he had a long face as full of pimples as a dried orange peel, and was excessively ugly, but he seemed quite self-possessed. He came out without uttering a word, slowly took up the guitar and casually tuned it, after

which he played a few tunes to which the audience paid
very little attention. Then he played a long piece, the
name of which Lao Can did not know; but towards the
end all the fingers were called into play and the melody,
high and low, quick and slow, moved people's hearts as
if there were dozens of strings and hundreds of fingers
playing in harmony. At that time there were incessant
"Bravos" from the auditorium, but the tune could still
be distinctly heard. After this piece was finished he
stopped, and an attendant brought him some tea.

After a few minutes a girl appeared from behind the
screen, who seemed sixteen or seventeen years old. She
had an oval face and her hair was gathered in a knot
on her neck; she was wearing silver ear-rings and a blue
cloth tunic and trousers, both with a yellow border;
but although her clothes were only made of coarse cloth
they were spotlessly clean. She sat on the chair on the
right-hand side behind the table, and when the accompanist took up the guitar again and started playing, the
girl stood up with the castanets in her left hand, holding them between her fingers and clashing them to the
tune played by the guitar, while in her right hand she
took the drum-stick and listened carefully to the
rhythm; then with one beat of the drum she burst out
singing. Every word was clear and every note was
mellow, like young orioles emerging from a valley or
young swallows returning to their nest. There were
seven words to every line, and some dozen lines to every
stanza. Some lines were slow and some quick, some
low and some high, while as for the variations in the
melody, they were innumerable. All other songs and
tunes that Lao Can had heard seemed inferior to this,
and he felt that she had attained the peak of perfection.

There were two people sitting beside him, and one whispered to the other, "I suppose this is White Sister?" But the other said, "No, this is Black Sister, her younger sister. She learnt all her tunes from White Sister, but she is much inferior to her. People can analyse her good points whereas they can't analyse White Sister's good points, and people can learn her good points whereas they can't learn White Sister's good points. All these years pleasure-loving people have learnt her tunes, and even the singsong girls have imitated her but at the most they can only sing one or two lines as well as Black Sister, while nobody can sing even one-tenth as well as White Sister."

As they were speaking Black Sister finished her song and went to the back. Then all the people in the theatre chattered and laughed and all the pedlars selling melon-seeds, monkey-nuts, fruit-jellies and walnuts, cried their wares, until the whole theatre was a babel of human voices. In the middle of this tumult a girl came out from behind the stage who was eighteen or nineteen years old. She was dressed in every respect like the other, and had a long, melon-seed shaped face, white skin and average good looks, appearing delicate but not seductive and distinguished but not disdainful. She came out with lowered head, seated herself behind the table, and clashed her castanets; and strange to relate, although these were only two pieces of ordinary iron, yet between her fingers they seemed instruments of great range. Then beating the drum softly twice she raised her head to look at the spectators, and her eyes appeared like autumn pools, like frosty stars, like pearls or black crystals kept in quick-silver. When she glanced right and left even the people far away felt that Little

Jade was looking at them, to say nothing of those seated near her, and thereupon the whole theatre became so still that even if the emperor himself had appeared there could not have been greater quiet. One could have heard a pin drop.

Little Jade then parted her lips and sang a few lines: the sound was low but indescribably sweet. All the organs of the body seemed smoothed as if by an iron, each into its proper place, while the whole body felt as if after drinking nectar, and there was not a pore that was not relaxed. After she had sung a few dozen lines she gradually sang higher and higher, until suddenly she soared to a very high pitch as if a steel rope had been flung into the sky, and Lao Can was secretly amazed. But even at that high pitch her voice could still circle and revolve, and after several trills it rose to an even higher note and ascended the scale for three or four notes more. It was like climbing Taishan Mountain from the Aolai Cliff on the west side: first you see the precipice reaching up to heaven, but when you attain the summit you realise that another peak is still ahead, and when you reach this you realise that there is yet another peak above. Thus with every turn the sense of insecurity increases, and as the sense of insecurity increases so also does one's amazement.

When Little Jade reached the highest pitch her voice suddenly dropped and, winding skilfully with all its art, seemed like a flying snake weaving its way down through the many ridges of the mountain and circling round and round in a very short space. Her voice dropped lower and lower until it gradually became inaudible, and all the people in the theatre held their breath in suspense and dared not make the least movement. In two or three minutes there seemed to be a small voice coming slowly out from beneath the ground to flare up again like foreign fire-crackers or like a rocket soaring up and multiplying into a thousand trails of coloured light before scattering down again. After this crescendo of sound many songs seemed to start all together. The accompanist also used all his fingers and played high and low in harmony with the voice, like many birds singing at dawn amid spring flowers, so that people's ears could not contain all the sounds and did not know to which melody to listen. In this medley they suddenly heard a final sound, and both voice and strings became mute, while "Bravos" sounded from before the stage like thunder.

After a little while when the tumult had begun to die down, a young man less than thirty years old in the front seat nearest the stage started to speak with a Hunan accent, saying, "When I studied in the past and read descriptions of good singers, it was said that the echoes of their songs would linger about the roof for three days but I would not believe it, thinking it was the writer's fancy — for how could echoes linger in the roof, and how could they hover there for three days? But since I heard Miss Wang sing, I realise how well the ancient scholars expressed it; for every time I have heard her I can hear her voice in my ears for several days, so that I cannot give my whole attention to anything I do. Indeed I feel that even three days is rather inadequate, and would rather use Confucius' words: 'For three months I cannot taste the flavour of meat.' Three months would be more correct."

All the people beside him said, "His comment is quite correct, and expresses our own feelings."

As they were speaking Black Sister came out and sang something and then White Sister came out again. Lao Can heard people say that the song she sang was called *The Tale of the Black Donkey* and was only about a scholar who saw a beautiful maiden passing by, riding on a black donkey. In order to describe the beautiful maiden the qualities of the black donkey were first enumerated, and when it came to the description of the beauty of the girl, there were only a few lines and the tale was done. It was all sung quickly, the speed increasing as it went along. One of Bai Juyi's poems contains the words, "Like big pearls and small pearls falling upon a jade disc," and these lines would apply to the excellency of this song. When she was at her quickest the listeners could not even keep up with her, yet every syllable was clearly enunciated, and there was not a single sound that failed to penetrate to people's ears: this was the wonder of it. Nevertheless it seemed slightly inferior to the last song. By this time it was only about five o'clock and people hoped that she would sing again; but if you want to know how good that song was, you must read the next chapter.

Chapter Three

IT is said that the people in the theatre thought that since it was still early Little Jade would sing for them again; but it was only her sister who came out and sang a few lines, and when she had finished everybody dispersed. The next day Lao Can felt some misgivings over his thousand taels of silver in the hotel, so he went to the main road where he found a bank called Sunrise, and sent eight hundred taels through the bank to his family in Xuzhou, keeping a hundred odd taels of silver for himself. From the shops on the street he bought a roll of silk and a length of flannel material for a gown. These he took to the hotel and called a tailor to make him a gown and jacket, for it was already the ninth month and, although the weather was still warm, as soon as the northwest wind started blowing he would have to wear padded clothes. So he gave the order for his new gown.

After lunch he went out of the West Gate to drink tea by the Bubbling Fountain. This Bubbling Fountain was the foremost of seventy-two springs in Jinan. It was within a large pool about an acre in extent, both sides of which were connected to rivers where the water flowed with a gurgling sound. In the middle of the lake three springs rose bubbling above the surface for two or three feet. According to local tradition they used to rise five or six feet, but later, after the lake was reconstructed, they had unaccountably become lower. The waters spouting out were thicker than barrels. On the north side of the pool was the temple of a local deity, and a matting shade was erected before it under which were five or six tables and a dozen benches where travellers might buy tea to refresh themselves.

After Lao Can had had tea he went out of the back door, took several turns to the east, and found himself at the Golden Fountain College. He went in through the second gate where there was a small well beside which the old scholar used to entertain his friends. Going further and passing another gate there was a hall skirted in front and behind by the lake, at the back of which were many banana plants, and, although their leaves were withered, the vivid greens still stretched far away into the distance. In the north-west corner among the leaves was a square pool of about twenty square feet, and this was the Golden Fountain, the second among the famous fountains of the city, the four most important fountains being the Bubbling Fountain just mentioned, this Gold Thread Fountain, the Black Tiger Fountain outside the South Gate and the Pearl Fountain in the governor's yamen.

According to tradition there was a gold thread in this fountain, but although Lao Can searched for a long time he could not find even an iron thread, not to speak of a gold one. Just then, however, a scholar happened to pass by, so Lao Can greeted him and asked him how the fountain came by its name. The scholar then took him by the hand and led him to the west side of the pool; there he bent down with head inclined sidewise, looked at the surface of the water, and said, "Look, there is a line at the surface of the water, like a floating thread, that makes a golden glitter floating on the top. Do you see it?"

Lao Can also inclined his head and looked carefully, then said, "Yes, I see it, I see it. Why is that?" After a moment's reflection he added, "Perhaps there are two springs beneath, striving against each other, so we see a line of light between them." "This fountain has been mentioned in books for several hundred years," said the scholar, "could it be that these two springs remained so long with their strength evenly matched?"

"You see how that line of light wavers to the right and to the left," said Lao Can, "that shows that there must be some discrepancy in the strength of the two springs." The scholar understood and nodded, after which they bowed and separated.

Lao Can went out of the college to walk along the city wall and when he passed the corner of the city he came to another street along which he walked in an easterly direction. There was a broad river outside the South Gate, the water of which was so clear that one could see the fish swimming beneath and the weeds, over ten feet long, swaying in the moving stream, forming an interesting spectacle. As he walked he looked about him and saw some large rectangular pools in the south, where there were a number of women standing on the stones by the pools washing clothes. He passed further on and came to another big pool south of which there were some thatched huts, and when he passed in front of them he noticed that one was a teahouse; so he went into the teahouse and sat by the north window, and a waiter brought him a pot of tea. The tea pots were made of earthenware and resembled those of Yixing, but they were local imitations.

When Lao Can had sat down he asked the waiter, "I hear you have a Black Tiger Fountain here. Do you know where it is?"

The waiter smiled and said, "Sir, if you go to that window and look out, isn't that the fountain?"

Lao Can accordingly looked out and saw just beneath his feet a tiger carved in stone, with a head about two feet long and fifteen or sixteen inches wide. A fountain spurted out with great force from the tiger's mouth, right across to the other side of the pool, and then the water flowed south into the river outside the walls. He sat there until he saw the sun was going down, when he paid for the tea, walked slowly back through the South Gate and returned to his hotel.

The next day he felt he had done enough sight-seeing, so he went on the street with his clapper. He passed the governor's yamen and in an alley on the west came to a fair-sized house, the gate of which faced south; while a piece of red paper pasted outside the gate bore the words, "Mr. Gao's house". A thin-faced man was standing in front of the gate, wearing a purple silk padded coat and holding a water pipe, looking much concerned. When he saw Lao Can he called out to him, "Sir, can you cure diphtheria?"

"I know something about it," replied Lao Can.

"Then please come in."

He went inside the big gate and turned to the west where there were three large chambers, elegantly furnished and with scrolls and paintings by contemporary scholars. In the middle there was a big scroll with a painting of a human figure, like someone moving in the wind, for the gown was billowing as if in a gale. The lines were excellently done, and on it was written in fine calligraphy "Mighty Wind".

They sat down and asked each other's names. That man was a native of Jiangsu, called Gao Shaoyin, a clerk in the governor's yamen, and he said, "My concubine is suffering from diphtheria. She has had it for five days and today she cannot even swallow water. I hope you will see whether she can still be cured."

"I cannot tell until I see," said Lao Can. So Mr. Gao ordered a servant to tell the people in the inner chamber that the doctor had come. Lao Can then went with him through the second gate, where he saw three more rooms, and when they passed the hall a maid-servant held aside the screen of the western chamber and said, "Please come in." He went in by the western wall and on the north side saw a big bed with a painted gauze net, and on the west side, in front of the bed, a small table with two stools.

Mr. Gao asked him to sit on a stool in front of the bed. A hand appeared from beneath the net and the maid-servant placed a few books beneath it to support it, after which Lao Can felt the pulse first of one hand and then of the other.

"The pulse is heavy," he said. "There is heat pressed by chill, which cannot come out; thus it has become serious. I would like to see her throat."

Mr. Gao then parted the netting and he saw a woman of about thirty, whose face was hectically flushed and who looked extremely weak. Mr. Gao lifted her up to face the light from the window, and Lao Can looked down her throat and found it swollen and practically closed up, besides being much inflamed. After he had examined it he said to Mr. Gao, "It was not a serious illness, simply a slight hot humour; but the doctors repressed it with chilly medicine so that the hot humour was unable to find a vent. Another reason is that she often loses her temper. Now you only need a couple of prescriptions of some medicine to cause perspiration and then she will be all right." Then he took from his medicine case a medicine bottle and a blow-pipe, and blew some medicine down her throat.

After that they returned to the sitting room and Lao Can wrote a prescription and gave it to Mr. Gao. The latter said, "Excellent. How many times should she take it?"

"Twice today," said Lao Can. "Tomorrow I shall come again."

"May I ask how much your fee is?" asked Mr. Gao.

"In my work I have no fixed fee," replied Lao Can. "If I cure the lady's sickness, should I be hungry at any time I will ask you for a bowl of rice, and should I be unable to go away I will ask you for travelling expenses, and that will be enough."

"In that case," said Mr. Gao. "I shall thank you altogether when she is cured. But may I ask where you stay? Then if there is any need I can send people to look for you."

"In Commissioner's Road, High Promotion Hotel," said Lao Can, and after saying this he went away.

After that he called every day, and in less than a week the lady was cured and regained normal health. Mr. Gao was overjoyed and sent him eight taels of silver; he also prepared a feast in the Northern Pillar Restaurant, and invited some of his colleagues in order to spread Lao Can's fame. Then one man told ten, ten men told a hundred, until there were officials and secretaries coming to invite him with sedan-chairs, and he had scarcely a moment's leisure.

One day when he had been invited to dine in the same restaurant, by another official, the man sitting on his right said, "Yu Xian is going to be the magistrate of Caozhou."

"He is not qualified for that by a long way," said Lao Can's neighbour on the left. "How could he be given such a position?"

"Because he knows how to deal with bandits," put in the man on the right. "After one year of his administration people do not dare pick things up from the roadside. The provincial governor thinks a great deal of him. The other day someone said to the provincial governor, 'Once I passed through a certain village in Caozhou and saw a blue cloth wrapper left by the roadside, which no one dared to pick up. When I asked the local people to whom it belonged and why nobody would pick it up, they said, "Last night somebody left it here." "Why didn't you take it?" I asked; but they all smiled and shook their heads, saying, "If anyone were to pick it up, his whole family would be doomed." Thus it seems that the ancient saying, "There was nothing taken from the roadside", has come true, and we are achieving that today.' When the provincial governor heard this he was very pleased, so he wrote a memorandum specially recommending him."

"Mr. Yu may be very able," said the man on the left, "but he is too cruel. In less than one year's time he condemned over two thousand men to death in the pillory. Could there have been no injustice there?"

"It goes without saying there must have been some innocent people," said the man beside him.

"The government of a cruel officer always appears impressive from without," said the man on the right. "Think of the case of Mr. Chang the Skinner, who was governor of Yanzhou and who was also like that. Things reached a state when 'none dared look him in the face'."

"It is true that Mr. Yu is cruel," remarked another, "but the people of Caozhou are really wretches. The year that I was magistrate there, there was not a day without a case of robbery. I kept two hundred police, but they were like cats who do not catch rats — completely useless. When the bailiffs caught robbers, they were either honest citizens or else people forced by robbers to look after their horses or carry their booty; while as for real robbers, they did not catch one in a hundred. Now Mr. Yu has acted like lightning and put an end to all robbery. Compared with him I feel rather ashamed."

"In my humble opinion," said the man on the left, "it is still better to kill fewer people. Although he is famous now, he will not escape retribution in future." After he had spoken the guests said, "We have had enough wine. Please give us rice now." When the meal was ended they all dispersed.

After another day Lao Can had nothing to do and was sitting idly in his room when a blue felt sedan-chair stopped by the door and a man came in, shouting, "Is Mr. Tie at home?"

Lao Can saw that Mr. Gao had come, and quickly went out to welcome him, saying, "Yes, yes. Please come in. Only my place is too humble and dirty for you."

"Not at all," said Mr. Gao. Then they passed

through the second gate where there were two chambers facing east. Inside his chamber, on the east side, there was a brick bed with bedding on it, on the north side a square table and two chairs, and on the west side two small bamboo cases. On the table were several books, one small ink-stone, a few brushes and a red ink case.

When Lao Can had asked him to sit down in the seat of honour Mr. Gao picked up a book at random, glanced at it, then exclaimed in surprise, "Where did you get this Song-dynasty edition of *Zhuangzi*? This edition disappeared from circulation long ago. Even scholars like Mr. Ji and Mr. Huang have never seen a copy like this: it is priceless."

"These are only some old books left by my father." said Lao Can. "They aren't worth anything. I just carry them with me on my travels to amuse myself by reading them like novels. It's not worth mentioning."

Then Mr. Gao looked round and saw that the other book was the *Poems of Tao Qian*, copied by hand in the Song dynasty by the poet Su Dongpo. It was the original manuscript from which Mao Zijin had printed his edition. Mr. Gao marvelled, and asked casually, "If you belong to a scholar's family, why don't you work for officialdom instead of pursuing this obscure profession? Although it is said, 'wealth and nobility are like floating clouds,' such an attitude is rather too eccentric."

"You are really over-rating me when you speak like that," said Lao Can. "It is not that I am not interested in officialdom, but my temperament is lazy and unsuited to worldly affairs. Moreover the proverb says,

'Those who climb high fall heavily.' I do not climb because I do not want to fall down too heavily."

"Yesterday evening," said Mr. Gao, "when I was dining at the governor's yamen, the provincial governor remarked that among our secretaries we had many scholars, and all those we knew were gathered there. But a certain Mr. Yao at the same table said, 'At the moment there is a scholar in Jinan whom you have overlooked.'

"The governor at once asked, 'Who is that?'

"Mr. Yao then told him how excellent were your scholarship and character, and how profound your understanding of human nature and experience in the world's affairs. The governor scratched his ear and chin with pleasure and asked me to send you a formal invitation immediately.

"'It may not be suitable for him,' I said, 'for he has not passed the examinations nor come to us specially, and we know nothing of his past qualifications; so it is rather difficult.'

"'Then you send him a private invitation,' said the governor.

"'If you were to ask him to come and cure sickness,' I said, 'he would not hesitate. But if you want him to join you as a secretary, it is not certain whether he will or not. You will have to ask him first.'

"'Good,' said the governor. 'You find out tomorrow. Then bring him to see me.' So I have come specially to discuss it with you. Would you care to come to the yamen today to see the governor?"

"That's all right," said Lao Can, "only to see the governor one has to wear ceremonial dress, and I am not used to it. Could I go in ordinary clothes?"

"Of course," said Mr. Gao. "We will go presently, and you can wait in my room. Then when the governor comes out in the afternoon we shall call on him in his office." Then he called a sedan-chair and Lao Can, wearing informal dress, went with him to the governor's yamen.

The provincial governor's yamen in Shandong was the former mansion of Prince Qi of the Ming dynasty, and in many places the old names were still retained; thus when you passed through the third hall it was called the Palace Gate: adjoining it was Mr. Gao's office and facing it the governor's office.

Lao Can sat down in Mr. Gao's room for a little while, and then the governor came out, a man of gigantic stature and benevolent appearance. When Mr. Gao saw him he went up and said a few words to him in a low voice.

Governor Zhang then called out, "Please come over, please come over."

An attendant officer cried, "His Honour wishes to see Mr. Tie."

Lao Can then went and stood before the governor. The governor said, "Delighted to meet you." Then he motioned with his hand and inclined his body, saying, "Please come in." The attendant officer had already drawn back the screen.

Lao Can went into the room and bowed low. The governor asked him to sit in the seat of honour on the red wood bed, and Mr. Gao sat facing him, while a square table was placed between them.

The governor sat down and said, "I have heard that your learning and talent are extraordinary. I am a man of little talent but by the grace of His Sacred Majesty I have been given this high position. In other provinces it is only necessary to discharge the routine work efficiently but in our province there is the river problem which is a matter of grave concern. In this matter I myself am powerless, but whenever I hear of talented people I always try to invite them in order to profit by their wisdom. If there is something you have noticed and you could instruct me a little, I should be most grateful."

"Everyone praises your good administration," said Lao Can, "that goes without saying. Regarding the river problem, whenever I hear people discussing it, they all seem to be following the ancient policy of Jia Rang, who said that we should not contend with the river."

"Isn't that right?" asked the governor. "You see how broad the river is in Henan, and how narrow the river-bed is here."

"That is not so," said Lao Can. "If the river-bed is too narrow to contain all the water, that is only during those days when the water rises; but the rest of the time the water flows slowly and that is why silt usually gathers here. You know, Jia Rang was only able to write good essays, but he never actually worked at river conservancy. Some hundred years after him there was another man called Wang Jing, who used the method handed down by Yu the Pacifier of the Flood. He believed in a policy of dredging and deepening, just the reverse of Jia's policy. For over a thousand years after he dealt with the river, there was no flood. Pan Jixun of the Ming dynasty and Jing Wenxiang of our dynasty also adopted his plan and thereby won great fame. I presume you know of it, too."

"What policy did Wang Jing follow?" asked the governor.

"He thought out his scheme from the record saying that Yu divided the river into nine tributaries and joined the streams together, basing his policy on the two words, 'dividing' and 'uniting'. In the later Han-dynasty history it is only mentioned that he had a dike every three miles to regulate the water. As for the details, they are too many to enumerate in a short time, but later I will write a memorandum on the subject for you."

When the governor heard this he was very pleased, and said to Mr. Gao, "You tell them quickly to clear the three rooms in the south, and ask Mr. Tie to move into our yamen, so that I can receive his instruction."

"I greatly appreciate the honour you are showing me," said Lao Can, "but I have a relative in Caozhou whom I wish to visit: moreover I have heard people discuss Mr. Yu's administration, and I would like to go and find out how good it is. After I return from Caozhou I shall come to receive your instructions." The governor was somewhat disappointed, but after speaking Lao Can took his leave, going out of the yamen with Mr. Gao to return to the hotel. If you want to know whether Lao Can really went to Caozhou or not, you must read the next chapter.

Chapter Four

IT is said that when Lao Can came out of the governor's yamen he left his sedan-chair and walked about on the streets enjoying himself for a little, spending some time in the curio shops, and only returning to the hotel in the evening. The hotel manager at once came to his room to congratulate him, making Lao Can feel quite bewildered.

"I have just heard that Mr. Gao came himself to invite you," said the manager, "saying that the governor wanted to see you, and you went to the yamen together. You really are in luck. Mr. Li and Mr. Zhang here have both got letters of introduction to the governor from the capital, but although they went four or five times they were not received, and on the rare occasions when they saw him they would be in a bad temper afterwards, cursing people and wanting to use their cards to send people to the magistrate to be punished. What great face you must have if the governor asks his secretary to invite you for a talk like that. You will certainly be given a position immediately. So of course I congratulate you."

"Not at all," said Lao Can. "They have been fooling you. I cured somebody's illness in Mr. Gao's family, and I mentioned to him that there was a Pearl Fountain in the governor's yamen at which I wanted to have a look. So today when Mr. Gao had leisure he asked me to go there to see the fountain. It was not the governor asking for me."

"I know what happened," said the manager. "Don't try to deceive me. When Mr. Gao was here I heard his servant say, 'When the governor went into lunch he passed Mr. Gao's room and called out to him, "After you have finished eating go immediately to invite Mr. Tie. If you go late he may be out, and you not see him today." ' "

"Don't you believe such nonsense," said Lao Can laughing. "It's not true."

"Don't worry," said the manager, "I'm not asking you to lend me money."

Then they heard someone outside shouting, "Where is the manager?"

The manager hastily went out and saw a man wearing a cap with a bright sapphire button and feather behind, dressed in soft boots, a purple felt gown and sky-blue jacket. In one hand he held a lantern and in the other a red visiting card, and he shouted, "Where is the manager?"

"Here I am! Here I am!" said the manager. "What is it?"

"Is Mr. Tie staying here?"

"Yes, yes," replied the manager. "He is staying in the east chamber. I will lead the way." Then the manager led him in and pointed to Lao Can, saying, "This is Mr. Tie."

The other went forward and knelt on one knee, presenting the card in his hand, and saying, "His Honour presents his respects to Mr. Tie. Tonight because the examiner has asked him to dinner he cannot ask you to stay in the yamen, so he told the kitchen quickly to prepare a feast and send it here immediately. His Honour says the feast is poor, and he hopes Mr. Tie will not be offended." Then he turned his head, and ordered, "Bring in the feast!"

Two men behind him carried in a three-layered hamper, and when the cover was removed they saw that the hamper was rectangular, the first layer containing small dishes, the second layer some large dishes including bird's nest and shark's fin, and the third layer a whole sucking pig, one duck and a plate of cakes. When they were opened and seen the man called out, "Manager!"

The manager was standing with the servants, spellbound, but when he heard the shout he quickly answered, "Yes, sir!"

"See that they are taken to the kitchen," said the other.

"I am sorry to have caused the governor so much trouble," said Lao Can hastily, and asked the man to go into his room to have a cup of tea; but he declined. However, when Lao Can insisted, he entered the room and sat on a stool on the lower side, but when invited to sit on the bed he declined emphatically. Lao Can took the pot and poured out a cup of tea and the other hastily stood up, knelt on one knee and thanked him, saying, "His Honour has ordered the Southern Library to be cleared immediately, and asks Mr. Tie to move in tomorrow or the next day. If you have any orders in future, just call me at the police station, and I will place myself at your service."

"You are too polite," said Lao Can.

Then that man stood up, knelt on one knee, and said, "I must ask leave to go back to the yamen to report. I shall be obliged if you will give me your card." Lao Can told the servant to give two strings of coins to the hamper-carriers, and at the same time wrote a receipt and saw the man out. The latter begged him not to escort him, but Lao Can still accompanied him out of the gate and saw him mount his horse before he returned.

When Lao Can came back from the gate the manager approached him with a broad smile, and said, "Do you still want to deceive me? Isn't that the governor's feast? The one who came just now, I hear, is Mr. He of the police station. He is a lieutenant general. During the last two years the governor has sent feasts to guests of ours on several occasions, but they were only ordinary feasts, and he only sent a policeman. This is the first time we have had such an honour."

"Never mind that," said Lao Can. "Ordinary or extraordinary, what shall we do with this feast?"

"You can either divide it to give to a few good friends," said the manager, "or write an invitation this evening for some honoured guests, and take it to the lake tomorrow to eat. Since this feast comes from the governor it is more precious than gold."

Lao Can laughed and said, "If it is more precious than gold, would anybody like to buy it from me? I will sell it for some gold to pay for my board and lodging."

"That does not matter," said the manager, "I am not afraid about that. It will be paid by other people. If you don't believe me, just wait and see if my words are true or not."

"All right," said Lao Can. "But regarding this feast, I think I had better give it to you to invite your guests. I don't want to eat such rich food."

They discussed the question for a while and finally decided that Lao Can should act as host and invite all the guests in the hotel to the outside room. Mr. Li and Mr. Zhang who stayed in that room were usually very haughty; but today, having seen how honoured he was by the governor, they had thought of nothing but how to make friends with him in order that he might recommend them. Now that Lao Can wanted to borrow their sitting-room to invite the hotel visitors they would naturally be honoured guests, and so they were delighted. All through the feast they praised Lao Can until his flesh crept, but he could do nothing and had to make polite conversation with them. So with great difficulty he got through the feast and they all dispersed.

But then this Mr. Zhang and Mr. Li went to his room to thank him again afterwards, and talked interminably one after the other, praising him for a long time.

"You can buy ranks," said Mr. Li, "first one this year and then another next spring; then in the autumn when you go to the capital, you will get a magistracy of the Taiwu District. This is very easy."

"Mr. Li here is the wealthiest man in Tianjin," said Mr. Zhang, "and if you can help him to get recommended, he will lend you the money to buy the rank. Then after you have got your lucrative post you can pay him back."

"I am very lucky to have you to advise me," said Lao Can, "but at the moment I am not anxious to be an official. Should I want to become an official in future, I shall come to you to beg your kind offices."

The two men after pleading with him again went back to their rooms to rest. "I meant originally to stay a few days," thought Lao Can, "but judging by this it seems that such entanglements will become more and more. As the proverb says, 'Out of thirty-six strategies the

best is to fly.' " Accordingly he wrote a letter that evening to Mr. Gao, thanking the governor for his kindness, and before daybreak he paid his bill, hired a cart
and left the city.

After he left the West Gate he went north for six
miles to a small town called Luokou. Before the Yellow
River joined the Daqing River all the seventy-two
springs of the city flowed into the river here, and it had
formerly been a very prosperous place; but since the
Yellow River changed its course only one tenth of the
former number of cargo boats passed there. When Lao
Can reached this town he hired a small boat to go to
the Lanzhou Harbour upstream, and as soon as he board-
ed the boat he paid two strings of coins to the boatman
to buy firewood and rice. Luckily there was a south-
east wind that day, and when the sail was hoisted the
boat was carried by the wind all the way. By the time
the sun set behind the mountains they reached Jihe
River where the boat moored and stopped. The next
evening the boat stopped at Pingyin and the third day
at Shouzhang, while on the fourth day they reached the
Dong Family Harbour. He spent that night on the boat
and at daybreak the next day he paid the bill and moved his baggage to an inn to stay.

This Dong Family Harbour lay on the main route
between Caozhou and Daming, so it had several large
cart stands. This inn was called the Dong Family Inn,
and the manager, whose surname was Dong, was over
sixty, and people called him Old Mr. Dong. He had
only one assistant whose name was Wang.

When Lao Can reached this inn it would have been
natural for him to hire a cart immediately to go to Caozhou; but because he wanted to find out more about the

administration of Magistrate Yu along the road, he travelled slowly to suit his purpose. It was nearly noon and even the latest risers among the travellers at the inn had already gone, so the assistant was clearing the rooms and the manager was making up the accounts, sitting at his ease outside the door. Lao Can also sat down on the bench outside the door, and said to Old Dong, "I hear your magistrate here is very capable in dealing with robbers. Just how good is he?"

Old Dong sighed and said, "The magistrate is an uncorrupted officer and he works with efficiency; only he is a little too relentless. In the beginning he caught a few robbers, but later the robbers learnt his temperament, and he became their weapon instead."

"What do you mean by that?" asked Lao Can.

"It takes a lot of explaining," said Old Dong. "In the south-west corner of our district there is a village called the Yu Family Village, where there are over two hundred families. There was a wealthy man in the village called Yu Chaodong who had two sons and one daughter. Both the sons were married, and he had two grandsons and his daughter was also married. This family was living in great comfort, but calamity overtook them. Last autumn the family was robbed, although actually all they lost were some dresses and trinkets worth only a few hundred strings of coins. They reported it to the magistrate, and after a very thorough investigation by him two minor robbers were caught, and several cloth garments recovered; but as for the robber chief, he had disappeared. Perhaps because of this arrest the robbers were angry. This year in spring they actually robbed someone within the city, and although the magistrate acted like lightning, for several days not a single robber was caught. Then a few days later another family was robbed, and after the robbery they even set fire to the house in broad daylight. Do you think the magistrate would put up with that? Naturally he sent his mounted police in pursuit.

"But after the robbery the robbers left the city with torches and foreign rifles in their hands, so who dared stop them? They went out of the East Gate, and after they had gone northwards for three or four miles the torches were extinguished. The magistrate led his mounted police in pursuit, and when they passed through the streets the watchmen told them the situation in detail, and the mounted police rode out of the city in pursuit. In the distance they could still see the robbers' torches, and after they had pursued them for about ten miles they saw torches again, and the robbers fired a few shots too. Naturally the magistrate was angry, but he was very bold, and he was at the head of some twenty or thirty mounted police, all carrying foreign rifles, so he had no reason to be afraid. They went straight on, guided by flickering torches and occasional shots. By the time it was nearly daybreak they were not far behind the robbers, and by then they had also reached the Yu Family Village. After passing the village they found there were no more shots being fired nor torches flickering, so the magistrate decided, 'No need to go on. The robbers must be in the village.'

"Accordingly they turned their horses back, came to the village and dismounted at the War God's Temple on the main road. The magistrate ordered his mounted police to despatch eight men with two horses in each direction, not allowing anyone to leave the village, and summoned all the local headmen. The day was then already bright, and the magistrate himself led his police on foot from the south end of the village to the north, searching every family. After searching for a long time they could find no traces of robbers, so then they started again from east to west, and in Yu Chaodong's house they discovered three locally-made rifles, several swords and about a dozen sticks. The magistrate was very angry, and said, 'The robbers must be in this family,' and sending for the local headman he asked, 'What family is this?'

"The headman answered, 'The family name is Yu. The old man is called Yu Chaodong; he has two sons, the elder called Yu Xueshi and the younger Yu Xueli: they are both scholars.'

"The magistrate immediately summoned the three men. You can imagine when countrymen see the district magistrate, and he in a towering rage, how can they fail to be afraid? When they came to the hall the three men knelt down, already trembling, and what could they say? The magistrate said, 'How dare you? Where have you hidden the robbers?' The old man was too frightened to speak, but his younger son who had studied for three years in the city and seen some society was slightly bolder. He straightened himself and answered, 'My family are all honest people, and none has intercourse with robbers. How can we have hidden robbers?'

" 'If you are not in league with robbers, where did the weapons come from?' asked the magistrate.

"Yu Xueli replied, 'Because last year we were robbed, and we often have robbers here in our village, we bought some long sticks and told our tenants and servants to come by turns to protect the family, and as the robbers all have foreign rifles, but we cannot get foreign rifles here in the country and did not dare to buy them, we bought several locally-made rifles from the hunters, to fire a few shots at night to frighten away thieves.'

" 'Nonsense!' roared the magistrate. 'Why should honest people keep weapons? You must all be robbers.' Then he turned his head and called, 'Bailiffs!'

"His followers answered with one voice, like thunder, 'Here!'

" 'Guard the front and back doors,' said the magistrate, 'and search them thoroughly.'

"The mounted police then started searching the Yu family, beginning from the inner rooms. They looked through all the cases and wardrobes, putting in their own pockets the lighter and more valuable trinkets. They searched for a long time without finding anything that should not be there, but in the end, in two rooms in the north-west corner where the broken farm tools were kept, they found a wrapper in which there were seven or eight garments, and three or four pieces of silk.

"The mounted police took these to the hall and reported, 'We found this wrapper in a room, dumped among other things. They do not look like their own clothes. Will Your Honour please examine them carefully?'

"The magistrate looked at the objects and frowned, and when he had fixed his eyes on them for a while, he said, 'These clothes strike me as belonging to that family which was robbed the other day in the city. I will take them to my yamen and check them up with the list.' Then pointing to the clothes he said to the three men, 'Speak! Where do these clothes come from?'

"The father and two sons looked at each other and were at a loss to reply, so Yu Xueli said, 'We really do not know where they come from.' The magistrate then stood up and ordered twelve police to stay with the headman to take the three men to the city for trial. After giving this order he went out, and his followers led over his horse. He mounted and returned to the city first with the rest of the police.

"Then father and sons and the rest of the family clasped each other and wept bitterly but the twelve police said, 'We have been riding all night and are famished. Quickly prepare some food for us and let us start immediately; for who does not know the magistrate's temper? The later you are the worse it will be for you.' The headman also went quickly home to tell his family and pack up his baggage. He told the Yu family to prepare several carriages, and they set out, only reaching the city when it was nearly midnight.

"Yu Xueli's wife was the daughter of a Mr. Wu in the city, who was an elected scholar, and she felt that since her husband and father-in-law and brother-in-law were all arrested, she should not stay behind; so she took counsel with her sister-in-law, saying, 'Now they have all been arrested, we must have somebody in the city to look after them. As for family affairs, I think you should attend to them, while I go quickly to the city to look for my father to find some way out. What do you think?'

" 'Very good,' said her sister-in-law. 'I was just thinking somebody must go to the city to look after them; but the villagers are all too countrified, and even if we sent several, when they reached the city they would behave like useless fools.'

"After they had spoken she put together some things, chose a swift two-horse carriage and went to the city, and when she saw her father she wept aloud. It was then only about ten o'clock and she was several miles ahead of the prisoners. Weeping she told her father their great misfortune, and when her father heard it he trembled in all his limbs and said, 'Now that you have come in the way of this Fury, it is very uncertain. I had better go there first to have a look.' So he quickly put on his clothes and asked for an interview at the yamen. But the gateman went up and came back, saying, 'His Honour says this is a case of robbery, and he will see no one.'

"Mr. Wu was a friend of the secretary inside, so he hastily went in to see him and explained the case. The secretary said, 'Under another magistrate there would be no question about this case; but this master of ours never judges according to the law. If it comes to my department I guarantee you their safety; but I am afraid it may not come to my department, and in that case I can do nothing.' Mr. Wu bowed to him several times and entrusted the matter to him. Then he went quickly to the East Gate to wait for them to arrive.

"After about as long as it would take to drink a cup of tea the mounted police came up with the carriage. Mr. Wu went forward and saw the prisoners looking ghastly pale, and when Yu Chaodong saw him, all he said was, 'Save me!', while his tears flowed down like a flood.

"Mr. Wu was just going to speak when the mounted police at the side shouted, 'His Honour is waiting at the court and has already sent several riders to look for us. Better go quickly.'

Then the carriage moved on; but Mr. Wu followed it and said, 'Take comfort. No matter what trouble you are in, I will do all I can.'

"As he was speaking they had already reached the yamen, and several bailiffs came out to hurry them, saying, 'Bring them immediately to the court.' Then other bailiffs came and put the three men in chains and took them up.

"They had no sooner knelt down than the magistrate threw down the list of lost property, and asked, 'Have you anything to say?'

" 'We are innocent!' was all the three men said.

"The magistrate banged on the table with his clapper and shouted, 'Confronted with the booty, you still say you are innocent? Put them in the pillory!' Then the attendant bailiffs dragged them away by force."

If you want to know what happened afterwards, you must read the next chapter.

Chapter Five

IT is said that Old Dong went on with his story, saying, "When Mr. Wu went to the district yamen to ask for an interview, his daughter, the wife of Yu Xueli, went with him to the yamen entrance and sat down in the Long Life Medicine Shop to await news. She heard that the magistrate would not see her father and that he had gone in to plead with the secretary, and she knew that this boded no good, so she immediately called in the head bailiff, Cheng Renmei, a well-known and able officer of Caozhou. She asked him to come over and told him of the injustice, begging him to do something.

"When Cheng Renmei heard it he shook his head, and said, 'This was a trick played by the robbers to revenge themselves. You have night-watchmen and guards in your family; how could you let the robbers plant the booty in your rooms without your knowledge? You really have been foolish.'

"Then she took off a pair of gold bracelets from her arm and gave them to him, saying, 'Anyway, you must help us. If you can save their lives we don't mind how much money we spend, even if we have to sell all our land and property and go away begging.'

" 'I will go and look for some way out,' said Mr. Cheng. 'You needn't thank me if I succeed; but don't complain if I fail, I will do all in my power, I can't do more than that. By this time they must have arrived.

The magistrate is already sitting in the court. I will go quickly and see what I can do for you.' Then he went away.

"When the head bailiff went back to the bailiff's office, he put the bracelets on the table in the middle of the hall, and said, 'Gentlemen, this Yu family case is certainly unjust. Let us all put our heads together to see if we have any way to help them; for if we can save their lives, in the first place it will be a good deed, and in the second place we shall all profit to the tune of several taels of silver. Whoever can think of a good plan can have this pair of bracelets.'

" 'There is no sure method,' all the bailiffs replied. 'We shall have to act as the opportunity arises, and do what we can.' When they had spoken their first act was to tell the other bailiffs standing by the court to look for an opportunity.

"By this time the three men had already entered the court, and when the magistrate ordered them to be pilloried some bailiffs came and dragged them away by force. Then the head bailiff, who was on duty that day, went up to the magistrate's table, knelt on one knee, and said, 'Your Honour, I beg to report that there are no spare pillories today.'

"When the magistrate heard this he was angry, and said 'Nonsense. I don't remember putting anybody in the pillory these last two days. How could there be no room?'

" 'There are only twelve pillories,' said the bailiff, 'and they have all been filled during the last five days. Will Your Honour please look up the record?'

"The magistrate turned up the record, using his fingers to count on the book, and said, 'One, two, three:

yesterday there were three. One, two, three, four, five: the day before yesterday there were five. One, two, three, four: the day before that there were four. There are no spare ones; you are quite right.'

" 'In that case could we put them in the prison first today?' said the bailiff. 'There are bound to be a few men dead tomorrow, and when there are vacant pillories we can put them in, Your Honour.'

"The magistrate thought for a while, and said, 'I hate these people. If you put them in prison they will live one day more. That would never do. Go and take down those four who were pilloried three days ago, and bring them here for my inspection.' So the bailiffs went and took down the four men, and dragged them to the court. The magistrate came down himself from his platform, put his fingers before their nostrils, and said, 'They have still a little breath.' Then he returned to his seat, and ordered, 'Give them two thousand strokes each. See if they die or not.' However after less than a few dozen strokes the four men all died. Then the bailiffs had no choice but to put the three men in the pillories; however they placed three blocks of brick under their feet, so that they could live for three or four days, while they hastily looked for other ways of saving them. But although they racked their brains to think of a solution, none would do.

"Yu Xueli's wife was indeed most devoted, and every day she went to the pillories to give them some soup to drink. After feeding them she went home and cried, and after crying she went to plead with other people again, knocking her head on the ground many thousands of times; but none could prevail upon the magistrate who was as obstinate as an ox. Yu Chaodong was advanced in years and he died on the third day, while by the fourth day Yu Xueshi was nearly dying. The wife took away the old man's corpse and supervised the funeral preparations, changing into mourning dress and entrusting the funeral of her husband and brother-in-law to her father. Then she went and knelt down before the yamen, weeping bitterly before her husband, and finally she said to him, 'You depart slowly, I will descend first beneath the earth to prepare your chambers.' So saying she took out a keen dagger from her sleeve, slashed her throat and died.

"When the head bailiff Cheng Renmei saw it, he said, 'Gentlemen, the devotion of this lady is good enough to be publicly commended. I think if Yu Xueli were taken down now he might still live. Therefore let us use this opportunity to go up and plead for him.

" 'Very well,' they all answered.

"Thereupon the head bailiff went immediately to look for the archivist and told him of the lady's devotion, saying, 'The people think this devoted wife has sacrificed herself for her husband, and are deeply touched. Could we ask the magistrate to release her husband in order to comfort the spirit of the lady?'

" 'Quite right,' said the archivist, 'I will go and see about it for you.' Then he snatched up his tall hat, put it on and went to the office, where he explained to the magistrate how devoted and heroic the woman was, and how all the people begged for a pardon.

"The magistrate laughed and said, 'Good. You have all suddenly become kind-hearted. You know how to be kind-hearted to Yu Xueli but will not be kind-hearted to your master; for whether he is guilty or not, if we release him he will not rest content, and I shall not be able to keep my post in future. The proverb says, "When you cut grass you must pull out the roots," and so it is here. This woman was even more odious, for she was obsessed with the idea that I had dealt unjustly with her family. If she were not a woman, even though she is dead, I would give her another two thousand strokes to vent my anger. You tell them outside that if anybody else comes to plead for the Yu family, we shall not need further proof of his being bribed; then you need not even report to me, but can put the man in the pillory also. That is all.'

"The archivist came out and related this in detail to Cheng Renmei, and sighing they both went their ways.

"In the Wu family they had already prepared the coffins for the funeral, and by the evening both Yu Xueshi and Yu Xueli were dead. The four coffins of the family were all placed in the Boddhisattva temple outside the West Gate, and when I went to town in spring I saw them too."

"What happened to the Yu family afterwards?" asked Lao Can. "Didn't they want to take revenge?"

"What could they do?" retorted Old Dong. "When people are unjustly treated by the authorities, what can they do but endure it? If you report to a superior officer, according to law he will send the case back to the district magistrate, and once it comes into his hands there will be another man condemned. Yu Chaodong's son-in-law was a district scholar, and after the other four had lost their lives Yu Xueshi's wife also went to town and thought of reporting to a superior authority; but older and more experienced people said, 'It is not safe; for who would go? If an outsider were to go, since he is not connected with the case he would at once be accused of meddling in other people's affairs; whereas if the mistress were to go what would happen to the two young grand-children and all the other household affairs to which she has to attend at home? If anything were to happen to her the property would be divided by the relatives, and then who would look after the two children? In that case the Yu family would come to an end.'

"Somebody said, 'The mistress certainly can't go, but if her son-in-law were to go, that would be all right.'

" 'Of course I am willing to go,' said the son-in-law, 'but it wouldn't help the situation: it would just mean another man dying in the pillory. For the provincial governor would certainly send the case back to the original district magistrate, and even if he were to send a commissioner to preside over the court, officials would always help each other. Besides, he has got the clothes and the lost property list as evidence against us. All we could say is that the robbers planted their booty there; but if they asked, "Did you see the robbers put it there? What evidence have you?" we should have nothing to say. He is an official and we are common citizens; he has the lost property list as evidence, and we have no evidence at all. Think for yourselves: how could we win the case?' Then they thought and agreed that really nothing could be done, so there the matter rested.

"Later I heard them say that when the robbers who planted the booty knew of this, they regretted it very much, and said, 'We bore them a grudge for reporting us and having two of our comrades killed; so we decided to hoist them with their own petard, wanting to give them a few months' trouble in which they would certainly have to spend one or two thousand strings of coins. But who could tell that it would come to such a pass that four of them would lose their lives? Actually we were not such bitter enemies.' "

When Old Dong had finished his story he asked again, "Now don't you think he was supplying the robbers with a weapon?"

"Who heard what the robbers said?" asked Lao Can.

"It was Cheng Renmei," said Old Dong. "Since the plea was rejected and the people died so pitifully, and they had received a pair of golden bracelets without doing anything, they felt rather uncomfortable; so they became more indignant, and all determined to find the robbers. There were also some local champions in the neighbouring districts who felt that the robbers had gone too far, so in less than a month they caught five or six robbers, among whom were three connected with other cases who were all pilloried and died; and two or three of them were only involved in this case, and they were released by the magistrate."

"This cruel official is really abominable!" exclaimed Lao Can. "Apart from this case, what other deeds of injustice has he perpetrated?"

"Countless others," replied Old Dong. "Let me tell you of a case in this village which was also unjust; but since only one man died, it did not seem so flagrant. I will tell you. . . ."

Just as Old Dong was going to begin, his assistant Wang called out, "Manager, what are you doing? We are all waiting for you to fetch the flour for dinner. Once you start talking you never stop."

When Old Dong heard him he stood up, went to the

back, got the flour and prepared the meal; then several small carts arrived in succession and gradually travellers came to the inn, and while Old Dong looked after them all he had no time to talk. After a short time they had dinner, after which Old Dong was very busy working out the various accounts and attending to business.

Lao Can was left with nothing to do, so he strolled down the street, and after he had walked twenty or thirty yards eastwards he came to a small shop selling oil, salt and groceries. He went in and bought three packets of tobacco, then sat down and looked at the man behind the counter, who was over fifty, and said to him, "May I ask your name?"

"Wang, of this district," he answered. "What is your name, sir?"

"Tie, from South of the Yangzi River," replied Lao Can.

"That is a good district," said the other. "As the proverb says, 'There is Paradise above and Suzhou and Hangzhou below.' It is not like our hell on earth."

"You have mountains and rivers," said Lao Can, "and grow wheat and rice, so what difference is there?"

The man sighed and said, "It is difficult to say." And then he fell silent.

"Is your magistrate good?" asked Lao Can.

"He is an honest official and a good official," replied the other. "Outside his yamen there are twelve pillories, and not one is unused any day. It would be rare to find one or two empty." As he was speaking a middle-aged woman came in from the back to fetch something, carrying a small bowl in her hand. When she saw somebody in the shop, she cast him a glance then went on with her search.

"How could there be so many robbers?" asked Lao Can.

"Who knows?" said Mr. Wang.

"I suppose many cases are unjust," said Lao Can.

"Quite just, quite just," said the other.

"I hear that whenever he sees anybody whose looks he doesn't like, he will put him in the pillory, and if a man speaks rashly when he falls into his hands he will also be killed. Is that true?"

"No, no," said the man.

During this conversation Lao Can noticed that Mr. Wang had lost colour, and his eyes had become red; while when he said "if a man speaks rashly" the other's eyes filled with tears, only they did not fall. But the woman who was searching for things looked away and could not help letting her tears fall, and abandoning her search, holding the bowl in one hand and hiding her eyes with her other sleeve, she ran to the back; and when she reached the courtyard she started crying. Lao Can wanted to question him further, but since he looked so sad he knew there must be something amiss and dared say no more; so he spoke of something else and left.

When Lao Can returned to the inn he sat for a while in his room, read a few pages and meditated for a time. Then he noticed that Old Dong was no longer busy, so he walked out slowly to chat with him, told him what he had seen in the small grocery shop, and asked him the reason.

"That fellow is named Wang," said Old Dong, "and his family consists only of his wife and himself. He married when he was about thirty and his wife was some

ten years younger; but after marriage they only had
one son, who would be twenty-one this year. The coarse
goods in their shop they used to sell in the village, and
when there was a fair they would buy something more
delicate for their son to take to the city to sell. This
spring when the lad was in the city it happened that he
had too much to drink, and talked carelessly outside
some shop, saying how foolish the magistrate was and
how he wronged people. He was overheard by some of
the magistrate's spies and they took him to the yamen.
When the magistrate ascended the court he simply cursed him, saying, 'How dare you spread rumours to
deceive the people?' Then he was put in the pillory and
he died in less than two days. That middle-aged woman
you saw was Mr. Wang's wife. She is over fifty now
and only had this one son without any other child, so
naturally she felt sad when you mentioned the magistrate."

"This magistrate certainly deserves worse than
death," Lao Can said. "How is it he has such a good
reputation in the provincial capital? If I had power he
would certainly be among those I would kill."

"Don't speak so loudly, sir," said Old Dong. "You
can say anything you like here, but if you talk like that
in the city, it may cost you your life."

"Thanks for the warning," said Lao Can. "I will be
careful." Then they had supper and went to bed.

The next day Lao Can said goodbye to Old Dong,
took a cart and the same evening reached Horse Fair.
This was a smaller village than the last, less than twenty
miles from Caozhou, and when Lao Can looked on the
street there were only three inns, two of which were
already full, while the door of the other was closed. Lao

Can pushed open the door and went in, but could not find anybody; however, after a long time a man came out and said, "We are not taking guests these days." And when asked the reason he would not explain.

Lao Can looked for a room elsewhere but the other inns were full, so he had to plead with this man, and finally the latter very grudgingly opened the door of one room, saying, "We have no hot water or food. Since you have no place to stay you can put up here, but our manager has gone to the city to fetch a corpse, and there is nobody else in the shop. If you want a meal or tea, there is a restaurant on the south side which is also a teashop where you can go."

"Thank you, thank you," rejoined Lao Can at once. "A traveller, you know, has to put up with anything."

"I am living in the room on the south," said the other, "by the door. If you want anything, sir, come and call me."

When Lao Can heard the words "fetching a corpse" it set him thinking. After he finished his supper that evening he went back to the inn, having bought some dry bean-curd preserved in tea, four or five packets of peanuts, and two bottles of wine, which he carried back. The assistant had already lit the lamp, and Lao Can said to him, "I have wine for you. After you have barred the door, come and have a cup."

The other consented very readily, ran at once to bar the door and came straight in and stood there, saying, "Help yourself sir, I won't take any." Lao Can made him sit down and poured out a cup of wine for him, and he was so pleased that he showed his teeth in a smile as he repeated several times, "Oh no, oh no," although actually the cup had already reached his lips.

At first they spoke of things in general, but after a few cups Lao Can asked, "Just now you said your manager had gone to the city to fetch a corpse. What did you mean by that? Was it somebody killed by the magistrate?"

"Since there is nobody here," said the assistant, "I can speak freely. Our magistrate is really a terror, a real devil. To meet him means death. It is his brother-in-law our manager has gone into the city to fetch. His brother-in-law was a very inoffensive person, and because the manager was so fond of his sister, they all lived in the back of this shop. His brother-in-law often bought a few rolls of cloth from the country looms to sell in the city at a profit to meet daily expenditure, and one day he went to the city carrying four rolls of white cloth which he put on the ground outside the temple. He sold two rolls in the morning, then he sold another five feet, and finally there came a man who wanted eight feet six, but insisted on having it from the uncut roll, saying, 'I will pay two cents more for each foot rather than have that roll which has been cut.' When the countryman saw that he could sell his cloth at a greater profit naturally he had no objection; so he cut it off for the customer.

"However, during less time than it would take to eat two meals, the magistrate, riding his horse, passed the temple, and somebody went up from the roadside and said something to him. The magistrate then looked at our manager's brother-in-law, and said, 'Take this man and his cloth to the yamen.' When he reached the yamen the magistrate ascended the court and ordered them to bring up the cloth, examined it and beat on the table, asking, 'Where did you get this cloth?'

" 'I bought it from the country,' he answered.

" 'How many feet are there in each piece?' asked the magistrate.

" 'From one of them I sold five feet and from the other eight feet six,' he said.

" 'Since you are a retailer,' said the magistrate, 'and the two reams of cloth are identical, why should some be sold here and some there? How is it you couldn't say how much there was left?' Then he ordered a bailiff: 'Measure that cloth for me!' When the cloth was measured the bailiff reported that one piece was twenty five feet long and one twenty feet six inches.

"When the magistrate heard it he was very angry and threw down a paper, saying, 'Can you read?'

"He answered, 'No.'

" 'Read it to him,' the magistrate ordered.

"Then a clerk at the side took the paper and read, 'On the morning of the seventeenth Mr. Jin reported, "Yesterday at sunset I was robbed five miles outside the West Gate. A man came out from the woods and attacked me with a sword, striking at my shoulder. He stole a string of four hundred coins and two rolls of white cloth, one twenty five feet long and one twenty feet and a half." '

"When this had been read the magistrate said, 'Both the measurements and the colour of the cloth coincide with those of the report. You must be the robber, and do you still want to argue? Drag him away and put him in the pillory. Then return the cloth to the original owner, and let him consider the case closed.' "

If you want to know what happened afterwards you must read the next chapter.

Chapter Six

IT is said that the assistant was relating how, when the inn-keeper's brother-in-law was carried off and put in the pillory, his cloth was given to that Mr. Jin and the matter was closed.

"It is clear to me that this must have been engineered by the bailiffs," said Lao Can, "and so, of course, your master has to go and bring back the corpse. But since he was innocent, why should people injure him? Hasn't your master found out the reason?"

"As to that," said the assistant, "as soon as he was caught we knew what it was. All the trouble came about because he was fond of talking. This is what I heard from other people: In a small alley in the city, at the west end of the main street by the South Gate, there lived a family consisting of only a father and daughter. The father was some forty years old, and the daughter about seventeen. She was very charming and unmarried. The father used to have a small business, and they lived in three thatched rooms inside a mud-walled court. One day the daughter was standing by the door when she was seen by Two-armed Wang, the chief of the mounted police, and he was so taken with her beauty that somehow he contrived to possess her. After some time, unfortunately, the father came home and discovered him, and he was so angry that he beat his daughter very severely and locked the main door, not allowing her to go out. But in less than a fortnight Two-armed Wang brought some accusation to make the father out to be a robber, so that he was put in the pillory and killed. Thus, later not only did the daughter become his wife, but that small house also went to him.

"Our master's brother-in-law used to sell cloth to that family and knew them, so he had heard of this. One day he drank a cup too much in a restaurant, and talked foolishly while he was drinking with Baldhead Zhang in North Street, saying, 'Why is it that these people have no conscience?'

"That man Zhang was also a foolish fellow, and he was interested in the story and took it up, saying, 'He is one of those Boxers, and many deities take possession of him, so I wonder why some of those spirits didn't restrain him?'

" 'Just what I was thinking,' said the brother-in-law. 'I heard that some time ago he called for the Monkey God, but the Monkey God did not appear, and the Pig God appeared instead. If he were not acting against his conscience why shouldn't the Monkey God come, instead of sending the Pig God? Since he is so unprincipled I fear one day the Monkey God may be angry; then he will raise his gold-plated club and strike him. That would be too bad for him.'

"So the two men talked on happily, little knowing that some members of the Boxer gang had reported them to Wang, taking careful note of their appearance. In a few months' time our master's brother-in-law came to grief, and Baldhead Zhang knew that he was in danger; but since he had no family he fled the next morning to Guide District to look for friends. Now the wine is finished I had better leave you to rest. If you go to the city tomorrow you must speak carefully. We people here live in a constant state of suspense, and if you make the least slip you will find your neck in the pillory."

Thereupon he stood up and picked up a half-burnt incense-stick to raise the wick of the lamp, saying, "I will fetch the oil-container to fill up this lamp."

"No need," said Lao Can. "Let's go to bed." So they separated and went to rest.

The next morning Lao Can packed his baggage and told the cart-driver to carry it to the cart, while the assistant saw him out and warned him repeatedly, "When you go to the city you really must not talk too much."

Lao Can laughed and answered, "Thank you for your warning." Then the driver started the cart and drove along the southern highway. By noon they reached the city of Caozhou and entered the North Gate. They found a hotel on the main street near the yamen, and he booked a room. A waiter came and asked what he would like for lunch, and he ordered a meal and ate it. Then he went to the magistrate's yamen to look around. He saw red silk hanging over the gate, and on the two sides there were indeed twelve pillories, but they were all empty without anybody in them; and he was surprised and thought, "Could it all be false, everything that I heard along the road?" Then he strolled about for a little while before going back to the hotel.

He saw in the upper chamber many people wearing tall hats wandering in and out, while in the courtyard there rested a blue felt sedan-chair, and many carriers wearing padded coats and trousers, also in tall hats, were eating unleavened bread. There were also men wearing uniform on which was written "Guards of Chengwu District", so he knew that the magistrate of

Chengwu must be staying here. After a long time he heard the servants in the upper chamber shouting, "Attention!" Then carriers promptly carried the sedan-chair to the steps, while those who held red umbrellas raised them up, and two horses were led out from the stables. Then the red felt screen of the upper chamber was drawn aside and a man came out wearing a crystal cap-button, embroidered coat and official beads, looking about fifty years old. He came down the steps and got into the sedan-chair which was immediately lifted up and carried out.

When Lao Can saw that man, he wondered, "Why is his face so familiar? I have never been in this district before; where could I have met him?" He thought for some time but could not recall the association, so he gave up thinking about it. Since it was still early in the day he went again to the street to ask about the administration of the district magistrate, and the answer was invariably "Good". Only the people all looked sad. He nodded to himself and felt that the ancient proverb "tyranny is more cruel than a tiger" was indeed true. Then he returned to his hotel and sat for a while at his door.

Just then the magistrate of Chengwu District came back, and when he entered the hotel he looked out from the window of his sedan-chair and his eyes met Lao Can's. By this time the sedan-chair had already reached the steps, and the magistrate alighted, his servants letting down the curtain of the chair and following him up the steps. Lao Can saw him at a distance saying a few words to one of his servants, who then ran towards his door and said to Lao Can, "Are you Mr. Tie?"

"Yes," replied Lao Can, "how do you know my name? Who is your master?"

"My master's name is Shen," replied the servant. "He has just come from the provincial capital, being appointed to the district of Chengwu. My master asks you to come over." Lao Can then remembered that this was the archivist, Shen Dongchao, whom he had met several times, but since he had not talked to him much he had forgotten him.

Lao Can then went up to see Mr. Shen and they greeted each other. Mr. Shen asked him to sit in the inner room, saying at the same time, "Excuse me, I must change my clothes." Then he changed his official robes for ordinary dress, and sat down, asking, "When did you come here? How long have you been here? Are you staying in this hotel?"

"I only came here today," said Lao Can, "having left the provincial capital about a week ago. When did you leave the provincial capital? Have you already been to your post?"

"I also arrived today," said Mr. Shen, "having left the provincial capital three days ago. All these attendants are escorting me to my district. The day before I left the capital I heard from Mr. Yao that the governor was very sorry when he saw that you had left, and said that he had always had great respect for scholars and thought that he could get them all; but now that he had met Mr. Tie who considered officialdom as floating clouds, he felt very humble by comparison."

"I have great respect for the provincial governor who admires talent so much," said Lao Can, "but I did not leave because I wanted to remain aloof. In the first place, I know well how slight is my talent and how superficial my scholarship, and that I do not deserve so much praise; in the second place, the district magistrate here has a great reputation, and I want to see what kind of person he is. As for retiring to an ivory tower, I not only have not the right to do so, but no desire either. There are very few men of talent in the world, and while people of the lowest intelligence may become recluses to hide their defects, if those who really have talent enough to improve society become recluses it is against the will of Nature who bestowed such gifts upon them."

"I have always had great respect for your profound observations," said Mr. Shen, "and today you make me bow down with even greater respect. No wonder that Confucius did not approve of the ways of ancient hermits. Incidentally, what do you think of the district magistrate here?"

"He is nothing but a cruel official of the lowest type, worse than the tyrants of history," said Lao Can.

Mr. Shen nodded his head repeatedly, and said, "We have been hampered in our observations, but you, travelling freely as an ordinary citizen, must know the truth of the matter. I suppose since the district magistrate is so cruel, there must be many cases of injustice. How is it then that nobody appeals to the higher authorities?"

Lao Can then related in detail what he had heard along the road, but he had only told him half the story when a servant came in to announce that dinner was ready. Mr. Shen asked him to stay for dinner, and Lao Can did not decline. After dinner he resumed his talk, and when he had finished he said, "I only wonder at one thing. Today when I was looking around outside the magistrate's yamen, I saw the twelve pillories all empty; so I wonder whether the country talk is unreliable."

"No, that is not the case," said Mr. Shen. "I have just heard from the magistrate of Heze that because the district magistrate was recommended yesterday by the higher authorities for promotion, and will be made an officer of the second rank, he has suspended punishments for three days as a public celebration. Didn't you see the red silk hanging outside the gate? I heard that the first day he suspended punishment — that was yesterday — there were still a few people not yet dead in the pillories, and they were put back into prison."

At this they both sighed, and Lao Can said, "You must be tired after travelling, and it is growing late. I had better leave you now."

"Tomorrow evening I hope you will come over again for a chat," said Mr. Shen. "I have a very difficult task, on which I want your advice. I hope you will not refuse it." After he had spoken they both retired for the night.

The next morning when Lao Can got up he saw the day was overcast, and although the north wind was not too strong he felt his padded gown very light on his body. After he had washed he bought some fried cakes for his breakfast and rather despondently wandered about the streets. He was thinking of going up the city wall to look at the distant scenery, when snow began to fall. Soon it was coming down very fast, whirling and flurrying, becoming thicker and thicker. He went back quickly to the hotel and told the hotel people to light a charcoal brazier for him. There was only one big piece of paper left in the window, and that half torn, so that it flapped and rustled in the snow and wind. The tiny shreds of paper at the side, although they made no sound, also fluttered incessantly, and the room seemed extremely cold and desolate.

Lao Can had nothing to do, for his books were still in the case and not easily accessible, so he sat there gloomily. Then he felt so deeply moved that he took out a brush and ink from the casket by his pillow, and wrote a poem on the wall about the district magistrate. The poem was as follows:

> *"Greed is in the marrow of his bones,*
> *Impatient to achieve renown;*
> *Thus injustice darkens the city*
> *And his cap-button is stained red with blood.*
> *Everywhere owls hoot,*
> *On every hill tigers roar;*
> *For killing his people as one kills an enemy*
> *This magistrate has become a general."*

Then he appended his name and his district, and after that he had lunch.

After lunch the snow was even thicker and, standing by the door looking out, he saw that the boughs and twigs of the trees seemed to be wrapped in new cotton. There were a few crows on the trees, drawing in their heads for fear of the cold, and ruffing their feathers for fear that the snow might gather on their bodies. He saw many sparrows sheltering under the eaves, also drawing in their heads from the cold. The sight of their hunger and cold was most pitiful, and he thought, "These birds depend on berries and tiny insects to satisfy their hunger; but now all the insects have gone into hibernation and cannot be found, while no berries will be left after the snow. Even if tomorrow the sky becomes clear and the snow melts a little, when the north wind blows the snow will turn to ice again, and they will still be without food and have to go hungry till next spring."

Thinking like this he felt moved with pity for the birds; but then he reflected, "Although these birds are cold and hungry for a season, nobody will shoot them or harm them, or cast nets to snare them. They are only cold and hungry for a season, but by next spring they will be happy again. But as for the people of this district, their crops have not been good these years; moreover, their magistrate is so cruel that he often takes them and punishes them as bandits, killing them in the pillories, so that they are too frightened even to speak. Thus they have fear in addition to their hunger and cold, so are they not worse off than the birds?" Thereupon he could not help shedding tears.

Then he looked again at the crows who suddenly gave a few cries, as if they were not complaining of their cold or hunger, but showing that they still had freedom of speech, and at that his anger surged up until he felt like having the magistrate killed immediately to vent his indignation.

His thoughts were wandering like this when a blue felt sedan-chair passed outside the door, followed by attendants, so he knew that Magistrate Shen had come back from paying his official calls, and he thought, "Why not write down what I have seen and heard in a letter, and tell the provincial governor about it?" Accordingly he took out paper and envelope from his case, and started writing; but no sooner had he begun than the ink on the ink-stone froze into solid ice, so that he had to warm it with his breath as he wrote. By the time he had covered only two sheets of paper it was already late, for when he warmed the ink-stone his brush became frozen, and when he warmed his brush the ink became frozen again, so that each time he warmed the ink he could only write four or five words, and in this way much time was wasted. Just as he was occupied like this the day became dark and he could not see what he was writing, for the sky was so overcast that it became dark earlier than usual. He called the hotel people to bring a lamp, and after he had shouted for a long time a waiter brought a lamp and came in, huddled up with cold, saying, "It's freezing." He put down the lamp and blew several times at the rolled paper spill he carried in his fingers before he could light it. The oil in the lamp had just been poured in, but was already frozen in coils like a snail, so when he lit the wick it would not burn.

"Wait for the oil to melt and it will be bright," said the waiter. He raised the wick and thrust his hands back into his sleeves for warmth, standing there watching the lamp, almost out. At first the light was no bigger than a pea, but gradually the oil reached it and it became as big as a bean. The servant suddenly raised his head and caught sight of the words written on the wall, and in great alarm he said, "Did you write this, sir? What have you written? You will get into trouble. This is no joke." Then he turned his head quickly to look outside, and when he saw there was nobody there he said, "If you are not careful you will lose your life, and we shall be involved too."

Lao Can laughed and said, "Don't be frightened. I have put my name under it. It doesn't concern you."

As he was speaking a man came in wearing a cap with red tassels, who called, "Mr. Tie!" The waiter went out looking rather dubious, while the man who came in said, "My master asks you to go across and have dinner, sir."

It was the magistrate's servant, and Lao Can said to him, "Please ask your master to start the meal, I have already ordered my dinner, and it will be here soon. Give my thanks to your master."

"My master says the hotel food is not good," said the servant, "and we have two pheasants sent to us which are already being prepared, besides some slices of mutton. And he asks you to come over and try the chafing dish. My master says if you really refuse, sir, he will order the dinner to be brought here. I think you had better go, sir. We have a big brazier in that room, four or five times as big as this one here, and it makes the room much warmer. Besides it is much more convenient for the servants serving the meal. Please oblige us with this favour." So Lao Can had to go over.

When Mr. Shen saw him he asked, "What were you doing in your room? It is very oppressive snowy weather; let us drink two cups of wine. Today somebody sent me some fresh pheasants, and since they are excellently cooked in a hotpot, I shall use this gift from another to entertain you." Then they took their seats and the servant brought in the sliced pheasant, some pink and some white, looking most appetising, and it was even more delicious when cooked in a hotpot.

"Do you notice anything special about these pheasants?" asked Mr. Shen.

"They have a peculiar fragrance," replied Lao Can. "Why is it?"

"These pheasants come from Peach Flower Mountain in Feicheng District," said Mr. Shen. "On that mountain there are many pine trees, and the pheasants are fed on the pine nuts; thus they have a peculiar fragrance. They are commonly called Pine Flower Pheasants, and they are not easily procurable even here."

Lao Can praised the pheasant, and then the servants brought in the dishes from the kitchen to go with the rice. When they finished their dinner Mr. Shen invited him into the inner room to sit by the fire and drink tea.

Mr. Shen suddenly noticed that Lao Can was wearing a padded gown, and asked, "In such cold weather why are you wearing a cotton gown?"

"I don't feel the cold at all," said Lao Can. "I have never worn fur since I was young, and I feel that a padded cotton gown is warmer even than your fox-skin."

"No, that is not good," said Mr. Shen. And he ordered the servant: "Take out my white fox-skin from that narrow leather chest, and carry it to Mr. Tie's room."

"There is no need," said Lao Can. "I am not being polite. Do you know of any street physician in the world wearing a fox-skin gown?"

"There is no need for you to sound your clapper in the streets," said Mr. Shen. "Why are you so eccentric? Since you don't look down on me, but consider me as a friend, I want to say something impolite, even though it may annoy you. Yesterday I heard you condemning those who are recluses, saying that talented people are all too few, and one should not think too lightly of oneself. I thoroughly endorse that saying, but your profession is against your sound opinion. The provincial governor urged you repeatedly to become an official, but you ran away during the night, insisting on coming away to sound your clapper. May I ask what difference there is between you and the ancient sage who dug a hole in the wall to escape, or the one who washed his ears and refused to listen to others? My words may offend you by their frankness but consider for yourself whether I am right or not?"

"Of course sounding my clapper does not help society," said Lao Can, "but does becoming an official help society? I would like to ask you a question. You are already the magistrate of Chengwu District, ruling over thirty miles and ten thousand people; but what have you done to help the people? I suppose you are confident in your heart, but will you tell me some of your policies? I know that you have been an official in two or three posts already, and may I ask what outstanding reforms you have accomplished in the past?"

"That's not fair," said Mr. Shen. "We ordinary people can only try to muddle along, but you have such great talent and wisdom that it is really a pity that you will not come forward to do public work. People who have no talent insist on becoming officials, and people who have talent insist on not becoming officials. This is the greatest pity in the world."

"On the contrary," said Lao Can, "I would say that it does not matter in the least if people of no talent become officials; the trouble arises when people who have talent want to be officials. Take magistrate Yu, for instance. Isn't he a talented man? But because he wanted to be an official at all costs, and wants to be promoted quickly, he acts against Nature and against principle. However, his reputation is so good that in a few years' time he will become a great official, and the greater he is the more harm he will do. When he governs a district he injures the district; when he governs a province he will cripple the province; and were he to govern an empire he would destroy that empire. Thus do talented people do more harm as officials or untalented people? If he were to knock about like me, sounding a clapper, people would not ask him to cure a serious illness, and if the illness were slight he would not kill people. Or supposing he killed one person by his prescriptions every year, then even if he were to be a physician for ten thousand years, he would kill less people than during his period of office as magistrate of this district."

If you want to know what Mr. Shen said to this, you must read the next chapter.

Chapter Seven

IT is said that Lao Can and Shen Dongchao were discussing the magistrate and how it was just because he was talented and wanted quick promotion that he committed so many acts of injustice; then they both sighed.

"Yesterday I said I had something important to discuss with you in private," said Mr. Shen, "and it is about this very thing. Consider, sir, what a tyrant this man is, and I have the misfortune to be under him. To work according to his wishes would be more than I could endure; but I see no means of doing otherwise. Now you are rich in experience, you have 'tasted all dangers and difficulties and know the people's heart', so you must have some good solution which I beg you to divulge."

"When you know the difficulty of a task, then it will be comparatively easy to perform," said Lao Can. "Since you ask for my humble opinion, may I enquire first as to your intentions? If you want to win the favour of your superior officers, impressing them and compelling their attention, then you will have to follow the example of the magistrate — that is to say 'force the people to become robbers'. But if you think of your position as one of trust and want to 'champion the people', there is another method which is to 'change the robbers into good citizens'. If your official status were slightly higher and you controlled a wider area, this would be very easy to accomplish; but when you have only one district, and that not a very rich one, then there are bound to be difficulties. Even so, it is not impossible."

"Naturally my aim is to 'champion the people'," said Mr. Shen. "If I can secure peace for my district, even though I am not promoted I shall not suffer from hunger or cold, and what is the use of increasing one's inheritance for one's children? But the emolument of this post is slight, and although my predecessor kept fifty police, even so there were many cases of robbery, so that he used too much official money, and that was why he lost his position. My feeling is that to spend money to secure peace for the locality would be worth while; but if I fail in this, my work will have been in vain."

"To keep fifty police would certainly cost too much," said Lao Can, "but with regard to your official salary, what sum could you raise without causing a deficit?"

"A thousand taels would not cause a deficit," said Mr. Shen.

"In that case," said Lao Can, "there is a way. If you will just raise one thousand three hundred taels of silver every year, and not interfere with my way of spending it, I will give you a plan and guarantee that you will not have a single case of robbery in your district. Or if you do, I guarantee that the robbers will be caught at once. What do you think?"

"If you will help me in this I shall be most grateful."

"It would be no use going myself; but I will tell you an excellent plan."

"But if you don't go," said Mr. Shen, "who will carry out your plan?"

"I am just going to recommend you a man," said

Lao Can, "but you must on no account slight him; for if you do he will immediately leave you, and then your case will be worse than before. His name is Liu Renfu; he is from Pingyin District and he lives in Peach Flower Mountain, south-west of the town. When he was some fourteen years old he studied boxing at the Shaolin Temple on Song Mountain. After some time he felt that although he had won fame he was not really proficient in the art, so he led a vagabond life all over the world for ten years, and when he was on Mount Emei in Sichuan he met a monk whose boxing surpassed all others; so he became his pupil and learned from him. He asked the monk where he had learnt his art and was greatly surprised when the latter replied 'At the Shaolin Temple'.

" 'But I was there myself for four or five years,' said Liu, 'and I did not see anybody who boxed well. From whom, then, did you learn?'

" 'Although this form of boxing comes from the Shaolin Temple,' said the monk, 'I did not learn it in the temple itself, for this form is already unknown there. Of the two styles of boxing you have learnt, one comes from Dharma, the founder of the school, and the other from his successor, Shen Guang. When they first taught boxing it was intended for monks only, so that by constant practice they might become healthy and vigorous; for when they went on pilgrimages in the mountains in search of holy men, they might meet wild beasts or robbers, and monks were not allowed to carry weapons; so they learnt this boxing as a means of self-defence. Moreover, with their sinews taut and their muscles firm they could better endure cold and hunger; for a travelling monk, wandering through wild mountains and de-

solate valleys in search of holy men, could not expect
to be provided with adequate food and lodging. That
is why the founders of Buddhism taught this style of
boxing. Later this Shaolin type of boxing became famous and many outsiders flocked to learn it; but these
people afterwards either became robbers or debauched
other men's wives, and there were no few cases of this.
Therefore the old monks of the last four or five generations have ceased teaching the real boxing, simply giving
demonstrations of some showy but ineffectual styles.
My boxing was learnt from a hermit in Hanzhong District, and if I practise it wholeheartedly, I shall attain
superhuman powers.'

"Accordingly Liu Renfu remained three years in
Sichuan and learnt all that the monk cou'd teach. That
was the time of the Taiping rebellion, and when he left
Sichuan he enlisted in the government forces. At that
time, of the two government armies one favoured
Hunanese and the other Anhui men, so that people from
other provinces were not fairly treated but only given
subordinate positions, in which they had no real power.
Liu Renfu belonged neither to Hunan nor to Anhui,
so nobody welcomed him, and in spite of his exceptional
gifts he was only given the rank of captain. Later,
when the rebellion was suppressed he had no inclination
to remain at his post, so he returned home and farmed
a few acres of land to support himself. In his leisure
time he would wander about the two provinces of Henan and Shandong, and all the people who studied
athletics in those two provinces knew his fame; but he
would not take any pupils. Even when he was certain
that a man was reliable, he would still be very reluctant
to teach him a few strokes. Not one of the athletes of

these two provinces was a match for him, and they all stood in awe of him.

"If you make this man your guest, give him a hundred taels of silver every month and let him spend it as he thinks best. He will probably only need some ten police to carry out his orders, each of them with a monthly salary of six taels of silver. The remaining forty taels will be enough for him to entertain guests. The three provinces of Henan, Shandong and Hebei, together with the northern parts of Jiangsu and Anhui, form one unit within which the robbers can be divided into two categories. There are the great robbers who have their leaders, their rules and regulations, and among whom are many able men; and there are the petty thieves who are amateur rogues and men out of work, who rob without plan, backing or proper weapons, and after a successful coup they either drink or gamble, so that they are very easily caught. If you take the robbers arrested by the magistrate, about ninety-five per cent of them are innocent people, and the other five per cent are these petty thieves; while as for the great robbers, not only their leaders but even their accomplices have escaped capture by the magistrate.

"Nevertheless, great robbers are easy to deal with, for those people in the capital, no matter whether they carry one hundred or two hundred taels of silver on their travel only need one or two guards to ensure its safety along the road. You might think that when there are such large sums of money, even if one or two hundred robbers joined together to plunder the convoy each could still profit very considerably. How is it then that one or two guards are a match for them? But there is a tradition among the great robbers that they must not molest these professional guards. So when these guards set out, they have their names put on their carts and they have to make certain signs along the road, and once these signs are made, even if they meet great robbers both sides will simply pay their respects to each other, but they will not come into conflict. The great robbers know all these professional guards, and the professional guards know all the haunts of the great robbers. When a great robber's friend reaches a place where there is a professional guard, he has only to make a sign and the guard will know where he comes from, and will have to entertain him with feasts; and when he leaves the guard will have to give him two or three hundred coins as travelling expenditure; while in the case of a great robber chief there has to be special entertainment. This is the law of the underworld.

"This Liu Renfu of whom I am speaking is very famous in the underworld, and the professional guards in the capital have invited him several times to join them; but he never would, preferring to remain in retirement as a farmer. If he comes to you and you treat him as your guest of honour, it will be like having a professional guard over your district. In his leisure time he will wander about in the teashops and restaurants, and will recognise immediately all those travellers who belong to the robbers' gangs. He will pay for a few dinners and teas, and in less than a fortnight all the great robber chiefs in the various districts will know that he is there, and they will immediately instruct their followers that since such a man is in that place there must be no disturbance there. The forty taels of silver left over every month, of which I spoke, is for this purpose. As for those petty robbers, they have no law and act upon the spur of the moment. There will certainly be people to inform of their whereabouts in nearby places, so that before those who have been robbed come to complain Liu's followers will already have arrested the culprits. Even if robbery is committed in more distant places, he will have his friends there too, who will arrest the robbers for him. Thus no matter where the robbers go, they will be caught. In this way Liu will only need some ten police, and in actual fact he will only make use of four or five of them; the other five will be to lend dignity to your official sedan-chair, or to carry out your commissions."

"What you have described is certainly an excellent scheme," said Mr. Shen, "but if he would not join the guards in the capital I am afraid that when I invite him he may not come. What shall we do?"

"If you ask him he certainly will not come," said Lao Can, "therefore I shall have to write a long letter on your behalf, begging him to save the lives of the innocent people of this district; and then he will come. Besides, we are very good friends, and if I ask him he will come to oblige me. When I was in my twenties I felt that the world was entering upon a period of confusion, so I looked out for talented men, and had many friends who studied military science; and when he was in Henan we were sworn friends, pledging that if one of us were asked by the government to take up office, we would enter public life together. At that time I had many different kinds of friends, some of whom studied political geography, some military science, some engineering and some athletics; and among the latter he was unequalled. Later we both realized that those who administer public affairs are a different type altogether, and all that we had learned was useless, so then we both turned to different professions to earn our living, casting our ambition into the Eastern Ocean. However, our former friendship still remains, so that if I ask him, he will certainly come."

When Mr. Shen heard this he bowed and thanked him many times, saying: "Since I accepted this post I have not had one night's sound sleep; but after what you have told me today I feel as if awaking from a bad dream or recovering from an illness, and count myself most fortunate. But what sort of man should we choose as messenger to take the letter to him?"

"You must have a good friend who is willing to undertake the hard journey," said Lao Can, "for if you just send an ordinary runner, it will seem as if you look down on him, and then he will not come, and I shall be blamed."

"Yes, yes. I have a cousin coming here tomorrow. I shall ask him to go," said Mr. Shen. "When will you write the letter? I should be grateful if you would write it quickly."

"Tomorrow I mean to stay in all day," said Lao Can. "At the moment I am writing a long letter to Provincial Governor Zhang, care of Mr. Yao, to inform him in detail of the work of the district magistrate here. I shall finish that letter tomorrow, and then I will have the other one written too. The day after tomorrow I am going away."

"Where are you going?"

"I want to go to Dongchang District to visit the private library of Mr. Liu Xiaohui, and see his Song and Yuan-dynasty editions. I shall go back to Jinan for the New Year, but where I shall go after that I do not know myself. The night is growing late; we had better go to bed." So saying Lao Can got up to go and Mr. Shen told his servant to light a lantern to see him back to his room; but when they lifted the screen the earth and sky seemed to have merged into one, for the snow had made everything white, and so bright was it that it dazzled the eyes. The snow beneath the steps had already fallen some seven or eight inches deep, making it impossible to pass. Only the path to the main gate was often swept, because people were constantly passing there; but the path to Lao Can's rooms could no longer be seen, for it was level with the rest of the ground. Mr. Shen quickly sent men to shovel out a path for Lao Can to go back to his room. When he opened his door his lamp was already out, and Mr. Shen sent him a candlestick and two red candles. He lit a candle and wanted to write a letter, but the brush and ink were frozen and refused to obey his orders, so there was nothing for it but to go to bed.

The next day, although the snow had stopped, the cold was even more intense. When Lao Can got up he ordered the hotel people to buy him five catties of charcoal and had a large brazier lit. He also bought several sheets of white paper and pasted up the broken window, so that after a little while the room became warm, unlike the previous day. Then he melted the ink, finished the letter he had started the preceding day, put it in an envelope and sealed it; he also wrote a letter to Liu Renfu and gave them both to Mr. Shen. Mr. Shen sent the first letter to Mr. Yao by special messenger to the post office; at the same time he put the letter to Liu-Renfu in the small casket by his pillow. By this time the kitchen had prepared a meal and they had their lunch and chatted for a short time.

As they were talking a servant came in to announce, "The second master and the secretaries have arrived. They are staying in the west wing, and when they have had a wash they will come over."

After a little while there entered a man of less than forty, who had not yet grown a beard. He was wearing an old blue silk fur gown, black fur jacket, and fur shoes soiled by the slush. This man came in briskly and greeted Mr. Shen, who introduced him, saying, "This is my cousin Shen Ziping." Then he turned and said, "This is Mr. Tie Bucan."

Shen Ziping came forward to greet Lao Can, and said, "How are you?"

"Have you had your lunch?" Mr. Shen asked.

"I have only just arrived," he said, "and came here immediately after washing, so I have not yet had lunch."

"Order the kitchen to prepare a meal for the second master," said Mr. Shen.

"No need," said Shen Ziping, "I will eat presently with the secretaries."

Just then, however, the servant came back, and said, "I have told the kitchen to send a meal over for the second master and the secretaries." At the same time another servant lifted the door screen and brought in some red cards. Lao Can knew that it must be the secretaries coming to see the magistrate, so he took his leave.

After dinner Mr. Shen again asked Lao Can to his room to explain to Shen Ziping in detail how to go to Peach Flower Mountain to invite Liu Renfu.

"What is the shortest route?" asked Shen Ziping.

"I don't know the best way from here," said Lao Can. "In the old days we used to go from the provincial capital along the Yellow River to Pingyin District, and about ten miles south-west of the district you come to the foot of the mountain. When you enter the mountain you cannot go by carriage, so you had better take a donkey with you; then in the easier places you can ride on the donkey, and in the more dangerous places you can walk. In the mountain there are two main paths, and some three or four miles along the western path you come to a temple. The Taoist priest in that temple knows Liu Renfu, and you can ask there to find out further details. There are two such temples in the mountain, one east of the village and one west of it; but I mean the one west of the village." When Shen Ziping had grasped these instructions they all went to bed.

The next morning Lao Can went out to hire a donkey-cart and packed up his baggage. While Mr. Shen was paying a farewell visit to the yamen he gave the fox-skin coat sent over the night before, together with a letter, to the hotel manager, telling him to give them to Mr. Shen on his return to the hotel, but not to send them before in case they should be lost. The manager hastily opened a wooden chest in his room and put in the coat, after which he saw Lao Can off to his cart, setting out to Dongchang District.

Then "feeding on wind and resting in dew" in two or three days Lao Can reached Dongchang, found a clean inn in which to stay, and made himself comfortable. The next day after breakfast he went out to look for a bookshop, and after some time he found a small bookshop consisting of three rooms, one side selling stationery and the other books. He went to the counter where books were sold, sat down and asked, "What books do you have here?"

"This is a cultural centre," replied the shopkeeper, "for this district is in charge of ten other districts, locally known as the Ten Beauties. All these districts are wealthy and cultured, and all the books they require are bought from us. Our shop is here, and we have a warehouse at the back, while we also have our own printing press. We do a good deal of printing here, so that we do not have to buy books from outside. May I ask your honoured name, and the object of your visit?"

"My name is Tie," said Lao Can, "and I have come to look for a friend."

"What is his name?" asked the shopkeeper.

"He is Mr. Liu Xiaohui. Formerly his father was the governor of our district, and I heard that he had a good collection of books, for he printed a catalogue of his books including many Song and Yuan-dynasty editions. I want to have a look, but I don't know whether it is possible or not."

"Of course I know the Liu family," said the shopkeeper, "it is the most important family here. Only Mr. Liu Xiaohui is already dead. His son, Liu Fengyi is a provincial scholar and at the moment he is a secretary in the Ministry of Finance. I heard that he has many books, but they are all stored away in big wooden boxes, probably to the number of several hundred boxes. They are all piled upstairs and no one ever asks about them. One of their relatives, a certain Mr. Liu, a district scholar, often comes round here; so I asked him once, 'What precious books are those in your family? Can you tell me anything about them?'

" 'I have never seen them myself,' he said.

" 'Are you not afraid they may be destroyed by insects?' I asked."

Just as the shopkeeper was speaking a man walked into the shop, pulled Lao Can by the sleeve, and said, "Go back quickly. A bailiff has come from Caozhou District, who wants to see you. You had better go quickly."

When Lao Can heard this, he said, "Tell him to wait, I will be back in a moment."

"I have been looking for you for a long time," said the other, "and our manager is very anxious. You had better go quickly."

"Never mind," said Lao Can. "Since you have found me now it will be all right. You can go now."

After the man from the inn had gone, the shopkeeper, who had watched him for some distance, said hurriedly to Lao Can in a low voice, "Have you valuable goods with you? Have you trustworthy friends in this district?"

"My baggage is not worth much," replied Lao Can, "and I have no trustworthy friends here. Why do you ask?"

"The magistrate of Caozhou is very fierce," said the shopkeeper. "It doesn't matter whether you are guilty or not, if he wants to put you in the pillory he will. Now since a bailiff has come from that district, it looks as if someone must have accused you. The outlook is black and discretion is the better part of valour. Since your baggage is not worth much, you had better leave it. It is more important to save your own life."

"Don't worry," said Lao Can. "He can't consider

me as a robber: of that I am certain." Saying this he nodded and went out.

Facing him as he left the shop was a small carriage, half filled with luggage and half with a passenger, and when Lao Can saw who was in it, he exclaimed, "Is that Mr. Jin?"

As he went forward the man in the carriage also jumped down and exclaimed, "Is that Mr. Tie? What are you doing here?"

Lao Can told him the reason for his visit, and said, "You ought to stop here. Better come for a chat in my hotel. Where are you from and where are you going?"

"It is growing late," said Mr. Jin, "and I have already rested. I want to travel further today. I have come from the north and am going home because there is some family business to which I must attend at once. So I cannot delay."

"In that case I must not detain you," said Lao Can. "Only let me ask you to sit down for a little. I want to write a letter to Liu Renfu, and I will trouble you to take it along for me." Then he bought a brush and several sheets of paper and an envelope from the stationery counter in the bookshop, and borrowing their ink he speedily wrote a letter and gave it to Mr. Jin, then bowed to him and said, "Excuse me for not seeing you off. When you see my friends in the mountains, please give them my best regards."

Mr. Jin took the letter and got into his carriage, while Lao Can returned to his inn. If you want to know whether the bailiff from Caozhou District had come to arrest Lao Can or not you must read the next chapter.

Chapter Eight

IT is said that when Lao Can heard from the inn-servant that a bailiff had come to look for him from Caozhou District, he was greatly surprised, and said to himself, "Can it really be that the magistrate considers me as a bandit?"

When Lao Can returned to the inn a bailiff came forward and bowed to him, placed a parcel on the chair beside him, and took out a letter from his pocket which he presented with both hands, saying, "With the compliments of Mr. Shen."

Lao Can took the letter and read it, and found that when Mr. Shen had returned to the hotel and the manager had given him the fox-skin coat, he was somewhat disconcerted; but then he decided the reason Lao Can would not accept it was because it was not in keeping with his manner of living, so he had chosen a sheepskin gown from a shop and sent it after him by a bailiff, and he wrote explicitly, "If you do not accept it this time, it will be too much."

When Lao Can read this he smiled and said to the bailiff, "Are you from Caozhou District?"

"I am from the Chengwu yamen, under Caozhou," replied the bailiff. Then Lao Can realised that the inn-servant before had forgotten to mention the Chengwu District. He straightway wrote a letter of thanks, gave the bailiff two taels of silver as travelling expenditure and dismissed him.

Lao Can stayed in Dongchang for another two days, and found that the books of the Liu family were indeed locked away in large cases, so that not only were outsiders unable to see them, but even members of the Liu family could not catch a glimpse of them. This depressed him considerably, so he took his brush and wrote the following poem on the wall:

> "This well-known scholar's family
> Has a library built up from the books of four families;
> But this collection in Dongchang District
> Is locked up in chests to feed bookworms."

After writing this he sighed and went to bed, and there we shall leave him for the time being.

On the day that Mr. Shen went to the district yamen to take his leave, he saw Magistrate Yu who exhorted him to use severe methods in suppressing disorder, and then after he had made some polite conversation the magistrate saw him out. When Mr. Shen returned to the hotel the manager very respectfully delivered to him the fur coat and the letter left by Lao Can, and when Mr. Shen read the letter he felt somewhat taken aback, so that Shen Ziping who was beside him, asked, "What has upset you, cousin?"

Then Mr. Shen told him that because he had seen Lao Can wearing a padded gown he had presented him with a fur coat, and he described their subsequent argument, saying, "You see, just as he was setting out, he left this coat behind after all. Isn't that rather ungracious?"

"You did not behave entirely correctly either, cousin," said Shen Ziping. "I think there are two reasons for his refusal: firstly, he thinks a fur coat too costly a gift for him to accept, and secondly, it is really useless for him, for he can't wear a fur coat with a cotton jacket. If you want to show your friendship you ought to send someone to get him a sheepskin gown and jacket, either of cloth or raw silk. Then if you send them to him by a bailiff he is sure to accept them. I don't believe he is proud or unnatural. What do you think?"

"Quite right, quite right," agreed Mr. Shen. "You tell a man to go and do as you suggested."

Shen Ziping saw that this was done, and despatched a bailiff to take the coat to Lao Can. Then, when his cousin had left for his new post, he hired a carriage from the district, and, taking little luggage and few attendants, he set out for Pingyin District. When he reached the district he hired two small carts for his baggage and a horse for himself to ride, and thus in one morning he reached the foot of the mountain. Here the horse could go no further, but fortunately there was a village at the mouth of the valley, with a small inn where people could sleep on the floor. Here he had to stop, hiring a small donkey from the villagers and sending the horse back; and after eating his lunch he set out for the mountain. As soon as he was out of the village he saw before him a sandy river more than a third of a mile wide, but most of the river-bed was filled with sand and there was only a trickle of water in the middle, over which the local people had built a wooden bridge a few tens of feet long. Although the river under the bridge was frozen over, one could hear the sound of water trickling through beneath the ice, sounding like the tinkling of jade pendants, and he knew that this was made by the water carrying tiny fragments of ice to beat against the larger pieces of ice. Beyond this sandy river lay the Eastern Valley.

The mountain here stretched from the south northwards, and in the middle were ranges of varying height. He could not see the whole mountain, but there were two ranges on the right and the left formed by two long undulating ridges which met at this point; so that in the middle was the summit of the mountain, on the left a big valley called the Eastern Valley, and on the right another big valley called the Western Valley. The streams in these two valleys joined together below to form one stream, and after three turnings one came to the mouth of a river which was the sandy river he had just passed.

When Shen Ziping entered the mountain and looked up he saw that at no great distance there were some high ranges in front, looking like a screen rising before him, where earth and rocks intermingled, interspersed with trees. It was just after heavy snow and the rocks were blue, the snow white, the leaves on the trees yellow; while there were green pine trees scattered here and there like the moss you may see in paintings. Riding his donkey and enjoying the mountain scenery he was exceedingly happy, and he thought of composing a few lines of poetry to describe the scene. He was just lost in thought when there was a sudden crash and he felt his legs slip, while he rolled over sidewise down into the gully. Fortunately the path lay alongside the gully, so that although he rolled down he had not far to go; moreover the snow on the two sides of the gully was very deep, and on the surface there was a thin layer of ice. As Shen Ziping rolled down, this thin layer of ice broke under his weight and he felt as if he were spinning down from a whirling mattress. After he had rolled some distance he was arrested by a big rock, in such a way that he was not injured at all. He hastily supported himself on the rock and stood up, his two feet making two great imprints in the snow, more than two feet deep. Then he looked at the donkey above him, and saw that its front legs were already freed, but its two hind legs were still embedded in the snow, unable to move. Thereupon he shouted for his attendants, but when he looked round there was no sign of them nor of the carts carrying his baggage. The reason for this was that there were very few people walking along this mountain path, so that although the snow was less here than elsewhere, it was still five or six inches deep. Thus the donkey was able to advance slowly without undue difficulty, the rider rapt in contemplation of the scenery, forgetful of the carts behind; but the carts had to be pushed up and met more resistance from the snow, so that although there was one man pushing and one pulling, each cart advanced very slowly, and they were now several hundred yards behind.

Shen Ziping was caught in the snow and could not move, so he had to possess himself in patience till the small carts should arrive. In about the time it would take to eat half a meal the carts came up, and all the men rested and tried to think of a way out. People at the bottom of the gully could not get up, and those who were up could not go down; so after much thought they decided the best way was to untie two ropes from the baggage and join them together, letting one end down for Shen Ziping to tie around his waist, while four or five men above together tugged the rope; and so at last they dragged him up. His attendants wiped away the snow on him, then brought over the donkey and he rode slowly forward.

Although the path was not too tortuous, it had sudden ups and downs, and the rocks were very slippery by reason of the frozen snow. Thus although they started at one o'clock and travelled till four o'clock, they did not cover more than three miles, and Shen Ziping thought, "I heard the villagers say it was about five miles to the village, but in three hours we have only covered half the distance." In winter the sun sets early, the more so in the mountain where there are ranges on both sides, causing the day to grow dark even sooner. So he rode and reckoned as he went, and the day had already grown dark.

Shen Ziping stopped his donkey and took counsel with the carters, saying, "The day is evidently growing dark. We have more than two miles still to go and the road is difficult, so that the carts cannot travel fast. What shall we do?"

"There is nothing we can do," replied the carters. "Fortunately today is the thirteenth, and the moon will be up early. At all costs we must get to the village. Probably there will not be any bandits along such a lonely mountain path; so even if we are late, it does not matter."

"Apart from the fact that there are probably no bandits," said Shen Ziping, "even if there were, I have not much baggage and I would not mind if they took it all. What I am really afraid of is that there may be wild beast. The day has grown dark, and if they should come out to devour us that would be a fearful thing."

"There are not too many tigers in this mountain," said the carters, "and they are under the control of a holy tiger, so that they never harm people. There are more wolves but if we hear them coming we can all take sticks in our hands, and then we need not fear them."

As they were speaking they came to a gully formed by a small waterfall whose water flowed into the valley. Although the waterfall was dried up in winter, this gully, more than twenty feet deep and about twenty feet wide, stretched across their path. On one side towered the sheer mountain and on the other yawned the deep precipice, so they had no other way. When Shen Ziping saw this his heart failed him, and he stopped his donkey to wait for the carts to come up. Then he said, "This is terrible. We have taken a wrong path and now we have reached a dead end."

The carters set down their carts to take breath, and one of them said, "Don't worry, don't worry. When we walked this way we didn't see any other path, so it can't be wrong. Let me have a look to see how we can cross this gully." He went forward for a few yards and came back, saying, "There is a way, only it is rather difficult. You had better dismount."

Shen Ziping dismounted and they led his donkey after them to where they could see that on one side of the big rock someone had built a stone bridge. It consisted of two slabs of stone, each only about a foot wide, and these stones were not closely joined, but there was an empty space of several inches in the middle, and the whole was covered with a layer of slippery ice. "This is terrifying," said Shen Ziping. "One false step will mean death. I really have not the courage to attempt it."

The carters looked and said, "Never mind, we have a way. It is a good thing we are wearing straw shoes and will not slip. There is no need to be alarmed."

"Let me try first," said one. Then he went over in leaps and bounds, crying out, "It's easy! It's easy!" He came back at once, and said, "We couldn't push the carts over. Let four of us carry one cart, and take them over in two crossings."

"Even if you can carry the carts across," said Shen Ziping, "I cannot possibly cross. And what can be done with the donkey?"

"Don't be alarmed," said the carters. "We will first help you over, and you can leave the rest to us."

"Even if you help me," said Shen Ziping, "I still would not dare attempt it. To tell the truth, both my legs have become limp, making it impossible for me to walk."

"There is another way," said one of them. "You had better lie down, and two of us will take your head and two of us your feet, and so we will carry you over."

"Impossible, utterly impossible," said Shen Ziping.

"I have a better plan," said another. "We will untie a rope and fasten it round your waist. One of us will go in front, holding the rope, and one of us behind. In that way you will feel safer and your legs will stop being limp."

"I suppose I shall have to do that," said Shen Ziping. So they took him over in that fashion, after which they carried the two carts over. Only the donkey would not budge, and after they had tried everything else they finally blindfolded it, and with one man tugging it and another beating it, they contrived to get it across. By the time this business was concluded, the shadows of trees were thrown all over the ground, and the moon was already very bright.

Having at last with great difficulty crossed the dangerous bridge, they had a rest and a pipe of tobacco before going on; but scarcely had they gone ten yards further when they heard two deep roars at a distance, and the carters exclaimed, "Tiger! Tiger!"

So as they walked they strained their ears to listen, and after a few more yards the chief carter stopped the carts and said, "Sir, you had better not ride that donkey. Better get off. Judging by the roar, the tiger is coming from the west and getting nearer. Probably he will cross this path, so we had better get out of the way; for if we wait till he comes it will be too late."

As he was speaking Shen Ziping dismounted from the donkey, and the carters said, "Let us sacrifice the donkey to the tiger."

Thereupon they fastened the reins of the donkey to a small pine tree on the path, and ranged the carts alongside. The men then went back some ten yards and hid Shen Ziping in a cleft in the rocks. As for the carters, some hid themselves under the rocks and covered themselves with snow, while two of them perched themselves on some high branches on the slope; all of them were looking towards the west when very swiftly something leapt out under the moonlight over the western ridge. When it reached the ridge it roared again and hurled itself down, so that it was already in the Western Valley. Then it roared once more. The men here were in a cold sweat and could not stop their teeth chattering; but their eyes were fixed on the tiger. When the tiger reached the Western Valley it stopped, and its eyes reflected in the moonlight were very bright; but instead of looking at the donkey it looked at the men in hiding. Then it roared once more and gathered its body in a spring to leap over the near ridge. Previously there had not been a breath of air in the mountain, but now a sudden gust swept the topmost branches of the trees, and dead leaves fell rustling to the ground, while the icy air seemed to cut into their faces. But the people here were by now so terrified that they had lost consciousness.

They waited for some time without hearing any sound from the tiger, so the two carters on the trees, who were the boldest, climbed down and called out to the others, "Come on out. The tiger is far away." Then the others emerged one by one from their hiding, and they pulled Shen Ziping out from the cleft in the rocks, dazed with fright.

It was a long time before he could speak, and then he asked, "Are we dead or alive?"

"The tiger has gone," they said.

"How did it go?" he asked. "Didn't it kill anyone?"

One of the men who had been on the tree answered, "I saw the tiger coming over from the west side of the valley. In one leap it soared over like a bird, and the place where it crossed was seventy or eighty feet higher than our tree. After it came down with another leap it reached the eastern ridge. Then it gave a roar and went east."

When Shen Ziping heard this he felt better, and said, "My two feet are still very soft and weak, and I cannot stand up."

"Aren't you standing already?" they all asked.

He looked down at his feet and realised that he was indeed already standing, so he laughed and said, "My body seems to be out of control." Then with people supporting him he made an effort to walk, and after some ten yards he began to regain control; but he sighed and said, "Although I did not lose my life to that tiger, if we come to another bridge like that we crossed just now, nothing will induce me to cross it. Besides, I am hungry and cold, and I shall surely be frozen to death." As he was speaking he reached the small tree and looked at the donkey, which was also grovelling on the ground, terrified by the tiger.

The attendants dragged the donkey to its feet and helped him on, then they moved slowly forward. Suddenly, turning round another rock, they came in sight of lights ahead and many houses, and they all cried out, "Good! Good! The village is in front!"

With this shout they all rallied, so that not only did the people feel their legs much lighter, but even the donkey did not seem as sluggish as before. In a very short time they reached the lights. But if you want to know whether Shen Ziping succeeded in finding Liu Renfu or not, you must read the next chapter.

Chapter Nine

IT is said that when Shen Ziping reached the village he noticed that it was thickly populated, and although there were not many shops there were numerous roadside stalls selling agricultural implements and the daily necessities of country life. He asked the country people the way to the temple and found Liu Renfu already there. They met and greeted each other, and Shen Ziping took out Lao Can's letter and gave it to Mr. Liu.

Mr. Liu took the letter and said, "I am a rustic man, ignorant of official rules and with little talent. I fear that I could not fulfil your cousin's expectations, so it would be better for me not to go. However I received a letter from Lao Can, brought by Mr. Jin, insisting that I should go; and since I was afraid that the Cypress Valley where I live would be too difficult for you to find, I stayed here to decline the invitation, and I hope that you will help me to decline it. It is not that I shirk responsibility or am over-proud, but I really feel that I may not be equal to the work and may spoil a worthy project. So I hope you will excuse me."

"Please do not be over-modest," said Shen Ziping. "My cousin felt that other people could not ask you to go, so he sent me here specially to invite you."

Then Liu Renfu realised that he could not decline, so he settled his private affairs and went to Chengwu

District with Shen Ziping, where Mr. Shen treated him as his guest of honour. Everything was done in accordance with Lao Can's instructions, and, while in the beginning there were one or two cases of robbery, after a month they achieved such a state of security that dogs no longer barked at night. But of this no more.

It is said that when Lao Can left Dongchang District, he intended to return to the provincial capital. One day he reached Qihe District and looked for a hotel at the South Gate, only to find that all the hotels on the street were full. He felt surprised and said to himself, "This place has never been so busy before. What can be the reason for this?"

He was wondering about this when a man entered the hotel, shouting, "Good! Good! It is nearly all through. Probably tomorrow morning we can cross over."

Lao Can had no time to question him, but he found the hotel manager and asked him, "Do you have any rooms?"

"We are full," replied the manager. "Please try another hotel."

"I have been to two hotels already," said Lao Can, "and they were both full. Try to squeeze me into a room; it doesn't matter whether it is good or bad."

"This place is really full up," said the manager, "but in the next hotel on the east side some guests left at noon, and if you go there quickly you may still find a room."

Lao Can accordingly went to the other hotel and asked for the manager, and there were indeed two rooms empty, so he moved his baggage in. The attendant came running to pour him water to wash his face, and put a lighted incense-stick on the table, saying, "Please smoke."

"Why is the place in such a hubbub," asked Lao Can, "so that all the hotels are full?"

"The north wind has been blowing for several days," replied the attendant, "and for the last three days there has been ice floating in the river, some blocks as big as houses; so that boats dare not pass, fearing to be wrecked on the icebergs. Already yesterday the upper river was completely blocked up with ice; below this bay boats could pass, but then they would be frozen up by the ice on both sides of the river. Yesterday His Excellency Mr. Li of Dongchang District came here on his way to see the provincial governor; but having reached here he could not cross the river, and became very anxious; so he stayed in the yamen and asked the local boatmen and headmen to break the ice. They have been breaking it all day, and it seems they are breaking through. Only they can't stop tonight, for once they leave off it will freeze up again. Our hotel was still full this morning, but we had a group of guests among whom was an old man, who looked at the river for a long time from the bank and said, 'They will never break through this ice; there is no point waiting here. Let's go to Luokou to see whether there is any other way or not. We can come to a decision there.' They only left at noon, luckily for you, for otherwise you would not have got a room." After saying this he went out.

Lao Can washed his face, made his bed, locked his room and went out to the riverside to have a look. He saw the Yellow River running down from the southwest to form a bay here, before flowing due east. The river here was not very wide, the distance between the banks being little more than half a mile, while the river itself was only some three hundred yards across; but the ice was piling up some seven or eight inches above the water. Then he walked some two hundred steps upstream and saw the floating ice from upstream floating down piece by piece. When it reached the bay here its passage was blocked by the ice in front, and, being unable to move forward, it stuck fast. Then the ice behind pressed forward, crushing against it with a grating sound, and this ice was impelled by the current to thrust its way by degrees to the top of the ice in front, so that the latter was gradually pressed down. Although the river was about three hundred yards across, the rapid current in the middle was only some hundred yards wide, and the water on the two sides was already frozen over, presenting a flat surface; thus, covered by the wind-blown dust, it looked like a sandy beach. But the rapid current in the middle kept rushing forward with a great uproar, forcing the ice which could not sweep past to leap sidewise. The ice on the smooth water, crushed by the ice hurtling from midstream, fled precipitately to the shore where it was thrown up for a matter of two yards, and many pieces of broken ice were forced erect under the pressure, standing upright like so many small screens. Lao Can watched this for about an hour until the ice was locked so fast that it could not budge.

Lao Can then walked further downstream, passing the place where he had stopped before and continuing further. He saw two boats with about a dozen men on board, all of whom were breaking the ice with great wooden pestles, pounding the ice before and then behind, while by the other bank there were two other boats similarly engaged. The day was growing dark and he decided to go back to his hotel, and then he noticed that the willow trees on the bank were already casting shadows on the ground and trembling in the wind, for by this time the moon had risen. He returned to the hotel, opened his door, called the attendant to light his lamp, had his dinner and went out for another stroll on the bank.

By this time the wind had dropped, but the frosty air stung even more sharply than the wind; however Lao Can had fortunately already put on the sheepskin coat given him by Mr. Shen, so that he could stand this bitter cold. He saw that the boats were still breaking the ice. On each boat there was a small lantern, and from the distance he seemed to see written on one *The Yamen*, and on the other, *Qihe District*, but he did not give them another thought.

He raised his head to look at the mountain in the south, glistening white and appearing even more magnificent in the moonlight, although the ridges were not clearly discernible. There were also white clouds gathering there which seemed to merge into the moonlight, so that only by gazing fixedly at them could one make out which were clouds and which mountains. For although the clouds and the mountains were both white and glistening, since the moon was behind the clouds their brightness emanated from within, whereas the brightness of the mountains was caused by the moonlight reflected on the snow, so that the effect was different. This was only the case, however, regarding the immediate vicinity, and as the mountains stretched further and further away towards the east, one could only see that the sky was white, the mountains white and the clouds white, without being able to differentiate between them.

Gazing at this scene of intermingled snow and moonlight Lao Can remembered the lines of Xie Lingyun:

"The bright moon shines on the gathering snow,
The north wind is keen and sad."

Only one who has experienced the bitter cold of north China can appreciate the appropriateness of the word "sad" in the second line. Now the moonlight flooded the ground with brightness, and when he looked up he could see no stars in the sky except for the Dipper in the north, showing like seven faint specks of white. The Dipper was on the west side of the Wall, with its bowl above and its handle below, and he thought, "Days have gone past like water flowing. In the twinkling of an eye the Dipper will be pointing east once more and another year will have passed. What will be the end, when year after year passes unprofitably like this?"

Again he called to mind the lines in the *Book of Songs*:

"There is a Dipper in the north,
But you cannot use it to pour wine."

"Now," he thought, "the country is in peril, yet the nobles and high officials are only afraid of being punished, and their policy is to let sleeping dogs lie, with the result that everything has come to a standstill, and what can the outcome be? With the country in such a state how can one think of one's family?" Thinking thus he unconsciously shed tears, and having no heart to en-

joy the scenery started walking slowly back to his hotel.
As Lao Can was walking, however, he had the impression that there was something on his face, and when he put up his hand to feel, he found two thin pieces of ice. At first he could not understand this, but when he realised he laughed, for these were the tears he had shed which had frozen instantaneously in the bitter cold, and there must also be some beads of ice on the ground. So he returned gloomily to the hotel and slept.

The next morning he went to the bank to have another look and noticed that the two boats used to break the ice were now icebound themselves by the side of the river. He questioned some men on the bank and found out that they had tried to break the ice for half the night; but when they broke the ice in front, the river froze up behind them, and when they tried to break the ice behind, the river in front froze up. So today they had given up the attempt. They would wait until the river had frozen hard, and then try to cross the ice, and this was what Lao Can would have to do also. Since he had nothing to do he went for a stroll in the town, and all he saw was a few shops along the main streets and a few tiled houses in the back streets, presenting a most desolate appearance; but since this was characteristic of most places in the north, he did not wonder at it. Then he returned to his room, opened his case and started reading a book.

After he had read for some time he again went to the door and stood idly there for a little while. He was just going to turn back when a servant wearing a red-tasselled hat came and bowed to him, saying, "When did you arrive, sir?"

"I arrived yesterday," replied Lao Can. But although

he answered, he could not remember whose servant this was.

The man seeing his hesitation knew that he did not recognise him, so he smiled and said, "My name is Huang Sheng and my master is Huang Renrui."

"Oh, yes, yes," said Lao Can. "My memory is poor. I often went to your house; how could I have forgotten you?"

"You, sir, are a person of consequence," said Huang Sheng, "and therefore could not remember us."

Lao Can laughed and said, "Although I am not a person of consequence, I really quite often forget people. When did your master come and where is he staying? I am at rather a loose end here, so I will look him up to chat with him."

"My master was sent by Mr. Zhang, the Chief Commissioner, to buy eight million pieces of timber in Qihe District. Now the timber is bought and the censor has gone through it, and he was just thinking to return to the province to conclude this business, when the river became impassable, so that he has had to wait for a couple of days. Are you staying in this hotel, too? In which room?"

"In that western chamber," said Lao Can, pointing to the west.

"My master is staying in the northern chamber," said Huang Sheng. "He moved in only the night before last. During the last few days he has been working, but since the censor left he moved here. Now he is in the district yamen having lunch, and after lunch His Excellency Mr. Li has asked him over for a chat. It is not certain yet whether he will be back for dinner or not." Lao Can nodded and Huang Sheng left.

This Huang Renrui was over thirty and a native of Jiangxi. His brother was a *Hanlin* scholar who had become a royal inspector and was a good friend of the War Minister Ta La-mi, thus Huang Renrui had been given a position as adviser in the Shandong River Conservancy. With a recommendation from the war minister he was given preferential treatment by the provincial governor, and after another recommendation he would become a district magistrate. He was a man of some taste, and while in the provincial capital he had been several times in Lao Can's company, so they knew each other.

Lao Can stood a little while longer at the door, then returned to his room, for it was now nearly evening. He read half a book of poems in his room until he could no longer see, and had to light his candle. Just then he heard someone coming in through the door, calling out, "Mr. Tie, I have not seen you for a long time!" Lao Can hastily stood up and saw that it was Huang Renrui. They greeted each other, then sat down and talked of what had happened since their last meeting.

"I suppose you have not yet had your dinner," said Mr. Huang. "Although someone sent me a hotpot and some dishes, I don't think they are very good; but this morning I ordered the cook to boil a fat chicken with mushrooms, and that should do for our meal. Better come to have your dinner in my room. As the old saying goes, 'It is rare to have an old friend come in a storm.' This river freezing is more tiresome than a storm; but now that I have come across an old friend like you I shall not feel lonely."

"Excellent," said Lao Can. "Since you have good

things to eat, even if you hadn't asked me I should have come."

Mr. Huang looked at the book on the table, took it up, noticed that it was the *Anthology of Poems of the Eight Dynasties*, and said, "This selection is not too bad." He glanced through a few poems then put it down, and said, "Let's go and sit in my room. So they prepared to go out. Lao Can straightened his books, took a key and locked his door, and went out with Mr. Huang to his quarters. He noticed there were three rooms, one bedroom and two sitting rooms. The door of the hall had a thick velvet door-screen. In the middle of the room there was a big table, and on the table a piece of rubber sheeting.

"Is dinner ready?" asked Mr. Huang.

"It will still be a little while," answered the servant. "The chicken is not quite done."

"Then bring the other dishes first," said Mr. Huang, "so that we can drink wine." The servant assented and went out, returning presently to spread the table with four pairs of chopsticks and four wine cups.

"Who are the other two?" asked Lao Can.

But Mr. Huang only said, "You will know soon."

Now the table was laid, but since there were only two chairs in the room the servant went out to fetch more chairs, and Mr. Huang said, "Let us sit on the big bed."

At the west end of the hall there was a big brick bed on which were spread mats, and in the middle of the bed was a tiger-skin rug on which had been placed a tray for opium. On the two sides of the tray were two wolf skins, and in the middle was burning a bright Taigu lamp. The reason that this lamp is called a

Taigu lamp is that in Shanxi there are many rich men, all of whom smoke opium, so the opium pipes and lamps in that district are of the first quality. Taigu is the name of a district in that province, and the lamps made in that district are well-shaped and bright, and may be considered the best lamps in the whole world. Unfortunately, this lamp was invented in China, for had it been invented in a foreign country the inventor would certainly have become famous and been praised by all the newspapers, and his government would have allowed him to take out a patent. China, however, has no such rules; so although the man who invented this lamp at Taigu and the man who invented the best opium pipe at Shouzhou did excellent work which is known all over the country, their own names remain obscure. Thus although one may say they spent their skill on unworthy objects, this is also a reflection on the state of society. However, let this suffice.

In the tray there were several enamel boxes, two bamboo opium pipes and two cushions, one on each side. Mr. Huang invited Lao Can to sit down, and lay down himself, taking up a pin to pierce a cake of opium which he baked over the fire, saying, "Do you still abstain from smoking? Of course it is not good if a man smokes so much that he wastes his time, but if one does not become an addict, just using it as form of relaxation, it is quite a pleasant pastime. Why do you refrain so scrupulously?"

"I have many friends who smoke," said Lao Can, "but none of them started smoking with the intention of becoming addicts, all taking it as a relaxation, until they found themselves addicts. By that time not only were they unable to use it as a relaxation, but it became a never-ending burden instead. I think you would do well not to relax yourself in this way either."

"I have my limit," replied Mr. Huang, "beyond which I shall not allow myself to be tempted."

As they were talking the screen stirred and two sing-song girls came in. The one in front was some seventeen years old, with a round face, while the one behind was a year or two younger and had an oval face. When they came in they curtsied to the men on the bed, and Mr. Huang said, "So you are here." Then pointing to Lao Can he said, "This is Mr. Tie, a friend of mine in the capital. Emerald Ring, you look after Mr. Tie and sit up there." Then the elder girl sat down on the side of the bed by Mr. Huang; but the younger one standing there was too shy to sit down, until Lao Can took off his shoes and moved further in, sitting cross-legged to make room for her. Then she sat down timidly on the edge of the bed.

"I heard they hadn't got this here," said Lao Can to Mr. Huang. "How is it that they have it after all?"

"You are right," said Mr. Huang. "They don't have this here. These two originally worked at Seven Mile Fair. Their proprietors belonged to this town, but their mistress stayed with them at Seven Mile Fair. However the other month their master died, so the mistress came back to town, and, fearing that they might run away, she brought them here as well. They don't do business here; but since I felt lonely I had them fetched. This one of mine is called Emerald Flower, and that one of yours is called Emerald Ring. They both have snow-white skin, quite ravishing. Look at her hand: I am sure you will be satisfied."

Lao Can laughed and said, "There is no need to examine her. What you say cannot be false."

Emerald Flower, leaning against Mr. Huang, said to Emerald Ring, "You bake some opium for Mr. Tie."

"Mr. Tie doesn't smoke," said Mr. Huang. "Let her do it for me." So he gave the pin to Emerald Ring who stooping baked the opium, filled the pipe and passed it over. Then Mr. Huang smoked it. By the time Emerald Ring started to bake again the servant had brought in the hotpot and the dishes, and announced, "Dinner is served, sir."

Mr. Huang stood up and said, "Let's drink some wine. It is very cold today." So he asked Lao Can to sit in the seat of honour while he sat in the place of the host, and the two girls sat at the two sides. Emerald Flower took the wine pot to pour wine for everybody then put it down and took up her chopsticks. First she helped Lao Can to food, and he said, "Please don't trouble. We are not newly married brides. We can feed ourselves."

Then she gave some food to Mr. Huang, and Mr. Huang gave some to Emerald Ring, who hastily stood up and said, "Please don't. This is too much honour."

Mr. Huang did the same for Emerald Flower, who said, "I will help myself." And receiving the spoon she carried it to her lips, barely tasted it, and put it down again. Mr. Huang asked Emerald Ring several times to eat, but although she answered, "Yes," she would not start.

Mr. Huang suddenly remembered something, and banging the table he exclaimed, "Oh, yes! Oh, yes!" Then he shouted, "Here." A servant came in from behind the screen and halted some six or seven feet from the table. Mr. Huang nodded to him to approach, and whispered a few words to him.

"Very good, sir," replied the servant, and went away.

After a little while a man wearing a padded gown of blue cloth came in, holding two guitars, one of which he gave to Emerald Ring and the other to Emerald Flower; and he said to Emerald Ring, "The gentlemen ask you to eat. Do as the gentlemen wish."

Emerald Ring appeared not to have heard clearly, and looked at the man, who said, "They ask you to eat. Don't you understand?"

Emerald Ring nodded and said, "Yes, I do." Then lifting her chopsticks she presented a piece of ham to Mr. Huang and another to Lao Can.

"Better not stand on ceremony," said Lao Can.

And Mr. Huang, raising his cup, said, "Let's drink a cup, and then let them sing two songs to accompany our wine." While he was speaking they had already tuned their guitars, and each in turn sang a song.

Mr. Huang stirred the hotpot with his chopsticks but could find nothing good to eat, so he said, "All the things in this hotpot have special epithets; do you know them?"

"No," said Lao Can.

Then Mr. Huang pointed with his chopsticks and said, "This is 'The Wrathful Shark's Fin', this 'The Never-bending Cuttlefish', this 'The Superannuated Chicken', this 'The Debauched Duck', this 'The Unyielding Pork', and this 'The Clear Soup'." The others laughed.

After that the two girls sang two or three more songs, until the servant announced, "The home-cooked chicken."

"We have had quite enough wine," said Lao Can.

"Let's have some rice while it's hot." The servant then brought in four bowls of rice. Emerald Flower stood up, took over the rice bowls and presented one to each person; and then they had some chicken soup with the rice, and all ate their fill.

After the meal they wiped their faces, and Mr. Huang said, "Let us sit on the bed again." The servant came and took away the rest of the dishes, and the four people sat on the bed. Lao Can leaned on one end and Mr. Huang on the other. Emerald Flower reclined against Mr. Huang, preparing opium for him, while Emerald Ring, sitting on the edge of the bed with nothing to do, took her guitar and toyed with the strings.

"I have not seen any of your poems for a long time," said Mr. Huang. "Today since old friends have met in strange surroundings you should write a poem for us to read."

"For the last two days, seeing the river frozen, I have been wanting to write a poem," said Lao Can, "but all your nonsense has sent my poem the way of 'The Debauched Duck'."

"If you are so 'Unyielding'," said Mr. Huang, "I shall become 'Wrathful'." Then they all laughed aloud.

"Very well," said Lao Can, "I will write one for you tomorrow."

"That won't do," said Mr. Huang. "Look at the wall. There is a place newly whitewashed, specially prepared for your poem."

Lao Can shook his head and said, "Keep it for yourself."

But Mr. Huang put his pipe down on the tray, and said, "Inspiration is too fleeting. I shall not let you off." So he got up and went into his room, coming back with a brush, ink-stone and piece of ink, which he put on the table, saying, "Emerald Ring, you grind the ink."

Then Emerald Ring poured out a little cold tea and started grinding the ink, and presently she said, "The ink is ready. You can start writing."

Mr. Huang took a duster and said, "Emerald Flower, you hold the lamp, and Emerald Ring, you hold the ink-stone. I will dust the wall." So he gave the brush to Lao Can, and Emerald Flower held the candlestick. Mr. Huang first jumped on the bed, stood under the place which was newly whitewashed and dusted it, while Emerald Flower and Emerald Ring both stood on the bed too, one on each side. Then Mr. Huang beckoned to him and said, "Come, come."

Lao Can laughed and said, "You really are a trouble-maker." So he stood on the bed, dipped the brush in ink from the ink-stone, warmed it with his breath and started writing on the wall. Emerald Ring feared that the ink on the stone might freeze, and warmed it all the time with her breath. The brush was nevertheless covered with a layer of ice, which became thicker and thicker until the poem was finished. It read as follows:

> "The earth is cleft asunder with the howling of the
>   north wind;
> Long slabs of ice rush down the darkening river.
> The ice behind pursues the ice in front,
> Attacking each other and struggling in rivalry.
> The river is swiftly ice-bound,
> A silvery bridge erected over frozen rocks.
> People longing to return home sigh,
> And travellers fret in vain.

> *Thus on account of a single river*
> *The carts cannot pass.*
> *Let us have girls and music and a fine feast*
> *To enliven this chilly night."*

Mr. Huang read it and said, "Good, good. Why not put your name to it?"

"Supposing we put your name?" suggested Lao Can.

But Mr. Huang said, "That would never do. I should be accused and lose my job for feasting with singing girls, only to get the name of a poet. It is not worth it."

Accordingly Lao Can signed his name and jumped down from the bed. The two girls put down the ink-stone and candlestick and warmed their hands at the brazier, and noticing that the charcoal was nearly burnt out, they added some fresh pieces. If you want to know what happened afterwards, you must read the next chapter.

Chapter Ten

IT is said that when Lao Can finished writing he lay down in comfort on the bed, and Emerald Ring, who had by now become less afraid of him, reclined by his side, asking, "Mr. Tie, where do you come from? What does this poem mean?"

Lao Can explained the poem to her line by line, and after a moment's reflection she said, "What you wrote is quite right; but can you write things like that in poems?"

"If you don't write such things, then what should you write?" asked Lao Can.

"When I was at Seven Mile Fair," she said, "I had many visitors, some of whom wrote poems on the wall, and I liked most to ask them to explain them to me. After I had heard a great many I found there were only two main themes: the comparatively superior people all said that although their talents were great, nobody in the world recognised them; while the others all described the beauty of some girl, and said how much they loved each other. Regarding those gentlemen's talents, we had no means of judging them; but it could scarcely be that all who came there were men of genius, without a single untalented person. So I made a silly remark, saying that if untalented people were so few, then, according to the proverb 'what's scarce is prized', oughtn't untalented people to be highly valued? Still, that's neither here nor there.

"As for those who described the beauty of girls, the girls they mentioned were all people we knew, and some of them hadn't even got properly formed noses or eyes. But if they didn't compare the girl to Xi Shi, then they compared her to Wang Qiang; and if they didn't say she 'caused the fish to sink to the deep and the swan to descend' they said she 'robbed the moon of its lustre and put the flowers to shame.' I don't know who Wang Qiang was, but I heard people say she was Lady Zhao Jun. Still I could hardly believe that Lady Zhao Jun and Lady Xi Shi could both be so ugly. That certainly couldn't be true.

"As for those who said how much the girl liked them and how dearly they loved each other, I was once foolish enough to ask one girl, and she told me, 'He stayed for a night and troubled me the whole night, so when it was morning I asked him for some silver. But he pulled a long face and shouted, "I paid the proper fee last night. What more do you want?" I said to him, "Of the money you paid, the hotel treasurer takes one part, the manager takes another part, and our mistress pockets all the rest, so that not a cent comes to us. But we have to pay for our rouge and powder and under-garments ourselves. We can't ask for anything from those gentlemen who only listen to our songs, only asking those gentlemen who stay the night for a tip for attendance." When I insisted like this, he gave me a small string of two hundred cash, throwing it on the floor, and cursing, "You bandit prostitutes, you baggages, you dirty bitches!"' Do you think that showed love? So I always thought writing poems very pointless, since it just means putting together a pack of lies. How is it your poems aren't like that, sir?"

Lao Can laughed and said, "Every teacher has his own method and every trade its own trick. My teacher taught me differently; that's why I don't write like that."

Mr. Huang had finished a pipe of opium, and putting it down he said, "It's certainly true that 'it is impossible to judge people from their appearance, and impossible to measure the ocean by pints'. Writing poems only means putting together a pack of lies, as this child has truly said. In future I shall never write poems again, in order to avoid putting together a pack of lies, to make myself a laughing-stock for them."

"Who would dare laugh at you, sir?" exclaimed Emerald Ring. "We are inexperienced country girls, and speak foolishly; so please don't be offended, sir, and I will kotow to you." Thereupon she turned herself to face Mr. Huang, and bowed to him several times.

"Who's blaming you?" said Huang Renrui. "What you said was really quite right, and no one has ever said it before. This shows how 'what is hidden from those concerned is plain to the bystanders'."

At this point Lao Can got up from the bed and said to Mr. Huang, "Thank you very much. I want to go back to my room now to sleep."

"Don't be in such a hurry," said Huang Renrui. "Wait till I have reasoned with you. Let me ask you this: can the ice on the river be broken through to-morrow or not?"

"It can't be broken through."

"If the ice can't be broken through, do you dare walk over it? Will you be able to leave tomorrow?"

"No," said Lao Can, "I shall not."

"If you can't leave tomorrow, have you any urgent business early tomorrow morning?"

"I have not."

"Exactly," said Mr. Huang. "In that case why are you in such a hurry to go back to your room? At such a gloomy and lonely time as this, to have a friend to talk with should really be counted as a joy in the midst of sorrow. Moreover these two girls, although they cannot be compared to peonies, are at least better than morning-glories, aren't they? Let us trim the lamp and pour out wine, and it will be very agreeable. I tell you this, in the provincial capital we are both busy, so that although we always want to have a good talk, we never find time for it; thus it was unexpected good fortune to meet you today when everything is just right for a good talk. I always say a man's most bitter portion is that he can't talk; yet there are people who think that a man can talk all day long, and wonder how I can say that he is unable to talk. The fact is that people speak in two ways: when they speak from the heart those are their own words; but when they speak from the throat that is just polite conversation. Now those people in the provincial capital are either my superiors or my inferiors; those who are my superiors look down on me so that I can't talk with them, and those who are my inferiors are jealous of me, so that I can't talk with them either. Still, you say, there must be some people who are on an equal footing with me; but even if there are people whose positions may be more or less equal to mine, at heart we are actually different, for some think themselves vastly superior to me and look down on me, while the rest think themselves inferior and therefore envy me. That's how I find myself unable to talk. One like you must really be considered as outside the common herd. Today I was lucky enough to meet you, for whom I have always had the greatest respect; so I think you should take pity on me and talk with me, but you insist on running away. A man can't help feeling sad."

"Very well," said Lao Can, "then I will keep you company. I don't mind telling you that if I went back it would only be to sit down; so why should I insist? It was because you had already invited these two girls and everything was right for you to talk sentimentally to them or make a few jokes and have some fun, so I thought my presence might embarrass you. But to tell the truth I'm no moralist who wants to eat cold pork and make sacrifice; so why should I be hypocritical?"

"It is just on their account that I want to consult you," said Mr. Huang. And standing up he pulled up Emerald Ring's sleeve, showing Lao Can her arm, and saying, "Do you see those stripes? Don't you think it's a shame?" Lao Can saw there were dark stripes and livid marks on her arm, and Mr. Huang said, "If the arm is like this I imagine the body must be in an even more deplorable state. Emerald Ring, let us see your body."

By this time Emerald Ring's eyes were already filled with tears, which, with an effort, she prevented from falling; but when he pulled her arm then many drops fell, and she said, "What is there to see? I am rather shy."

"Isn't the child stupid!" exclaimed Mr. Huang. "What is there to be afraid of if we look? How can you be shy when you are in this profession?"

"Why not?" asked Emerald Ring.

By now there were tears in Emerald Flower's eyes too, and she said, "Don't ask her to take off her clothes." Then turning her head she whispered something softly to Mr. Huang, who nodded his head and did not insist.

During this time Lao Can had stretched himself on the bed and was thinking, "These are both people's beloved children, and when their parents looked after them who knows how much loving care they lavished on them, to what trouble they went, or how much they suffered for them. Even when they hurt themselves through naughtiness they would be caressed, and not only would their parents caress them but also feel grieved at heart; while if they were beaten by other children their parents' indignation would know no bounds. Such love and compassion cannot be expressed in words. Then, who knows, when they had brought them up, either because there was famine that year, or because the father smoked opium or gambled or had a lawsuit, they reached such a pitch of desperation that, not knowing what they did, they sold their daughters to these houses, to be maltreated by these procuresses and suffer indescribable hardships." Then he called to mind all that he had heard and seen of the cruelty of procuresses in various places; for they seemed to have come all from one school, where they had learnt the same cruelty. At this he became so indignant that he could not prevent his own eyes feeling a little moist.

At this moment, when they were all silent without a word, Mr. Huang's servant led in someone carrying baggage into the inner room. Then he came out and said to Mr. Huang, "Sir, would you ask for Mr. Tie's key, so that we can take Emerald Ring's bedding in?"

"Naturally it should be taken to your master's room," said Lao Can.

"All right, all right," said Mr. Huang, "don't be a moralist. Give me your key."

"No, I will not," said Lao Can. "I never do that."

"I have already given the order and paid for it," said Mr. Huang. "Why be so obstinate?"

"It doesn't matter about the payment; I will return you the amount tomorrow," said Lao Can. "And since it is paid, the procuress will have nothing to say, and cannot blame the girl; so what is there to be afraid of?"

"If you really send her back," said Emerald Flower, "she will not escape a sound beating; for it will be said that she offended the guest."

"In that case I have another suggestion," said Lao Can. "Send her back today and tell her that tomorrow we want her again, that will be all right. Anyway, she was ordered by Mr. Huang, so what has it to do with me? I am willing to pay for it. Isn't that simple?"

"I ordered her for you," said Mr. Huang. "I kept Emerald Flower here last night already, so how can I send her back today? We just want them to cheer us up. I don't insist on your doing anything. Last night Emerald Flower talked to me all night in my room, and we sat till morning. She can cheer you up and at the same time she will escape a beating; wouldn't that be a good thing? Because they have their rule that if they are not kept for the night, they must not take a meal. Thus if they return before dark they have to sit half the night hungry, and probably will be beaten into the bargain, because their mistress will always say, 'If the client keeps you so long, he must be fond of you. Why then does he send you back? You must have failed to please him.' Then if they are unlucky they will be beaten. So I told them to say that they were to be kept for the night. Didn't you notice that attendant telling Emerald Ring to eat? That is their sign."

After he had spoken Emerald Flower said to Emerald Ring, "You plead with Mr. Tie to take pity on you."

"I shall still pay the sum of money and send her back," said Lao Can, "for no other reason but that she may have peace and I may have peace."

Emerald Flower gave a little snort, and said, "It is true that you may have peace, but she certainly will not."

Then Emerald Ring turned herself to face Lao Can, and said, "Mr. Tie, you seem so kind; why won't you be kind to us children? The bed in your room is twelve feet wide, and your bedding only takes three feet, still leaving nine feet empty. Couldn't you give some to me as a refuge for a night? If you condescend to want my attendance, I can serve you opium and tea; and even if you find me very disagreeable I hope you will allow me to pass a night on the corner of your bed as a great favour."

At this Lao Can took the key out of his pocket and gave it to Emerald Flower, saying, "You can do as you like; only don't touch my bedding."

Emerald Flower stood up and gave the key to the servant, saying, "Thank you very much. See that the man takes the bedding in and comes out; then please lock up the room. Thank you very, very much." The servant took the key and went out.

Lao Can patted Emerald Ring's cheek and asked,

"What district are you from? What is the name of your mistress, and when were you sold to her?"

"My mistress is called Zhang," said Emerald Ring. After she had said this she stopped, took her handkerchief out of her sleeve to wipe her tears, and wiped and wiped, unable to speak.

"Don't cry," said Lao Can. "I asked about your family in order to cheer you up. You don't have to talk about it unless you want to. Why become so sad?"

"I have no family," said Emerald Ring.

"Don't be angry, sir," said Emerald Flower. "This child's temper is bad, so that she often gets beaten; but actually she has reason to be sad. Two years ago her family was very wealthy, but last year she was sold here, and because she had never suffered much when she was young she could not please people; although actually our mistress is one of the best of her kind, and by next year she won't have such a good time as she is having now."

By this time Emerald Ring had covered her face and begun crying and Emerald Flower shouted at her, "This child evidently doesn't want to go on living! The gentlemen order you here to cheer them up, and you start crying yourself. Won't that make the gentlemen angry? You'd better stop."

"Don't stop her," said Lao Can. "It's good for her to cry. She has been feeling wronged all this time without any place to cry; but today she has fortunately met us who are kind-hearted, and she can cry her fill until she feels more comfortable." Then he patted Emerald Ring's shoulder and said, "It doesn't matter if you cry out loud. I know Mr. Huang is not superstitious. You cry as much as you like."

Mr. Huang beside him shouted, "Emerald Ring, good girl, go on crying! I shall be grateful if you cry away all my sorrows too!" When they heard this they all laughed, and even Emerald Ring, covering her face, laughed too.

The truth was that Emerald Ring knew that before clients one must not cry, but when Lao Can asked about her family, and Emerald Flower mentioned that two years before she was still wealthy, it made her so sad that her tears began to fall and she could not stop them. When she heard Lao Can say, "She has been sad all this time without any place to cry, let her cry her fill until she feels more comfortable," she thought, "Since I fell into misfortune no one has been so considerate. It shows that not all men treat women like dirt; only I don't know how many men there are like this in the world — it would be pleasant to meet a few in my life, for since I have met one there must be others." Thinking like this she forgot all her sorrow, and she was just turning her head to hear what they were saying when suddenly Mr. Huang called out asking her to cry for him, which sounded very funny. So with tears in her eyes she laughed, raising her head to look at Mr. Huang; and when the others saw her like this they could not help laughing too. Emerald Ring's heart at this moment was in utter confusion, and seeing them laugh hysterically, she laughed hysterically with them.

Then Lao Can said, "Now that we have cried and laughed I would still like to know how she was wealthy two years ago. Emerald Flower, you tell me."

"She is from Jidong District," said Emerald Flower. "Her family was named Tian and lived outside the South Gate of the district, where they possessed some two hundred acres of land, and they also had a grocery shop in the town. Her parents had no other children but her and her younger brother, who is five years old this year, and there was also a grandmother. The land by that Daqing River is mainly planted with cotton, and each acre is worth over a hundred strings of cash. They possessed more than two hundred acres, worth more than twenty thousand strings of cash, and together with the shop their property was worth more than three hundred thousand. The proverb says, 'With ten thousand strings of cash one can be considered wealthy.' They had three hundred thousand strings, so shouldn't that be considered very wealthy?"

"If her family had thirty thousand strings' worth of property," said Lao Can, "they were very well off. How could they become poor, and poor to that extent?"

"It all happened in a flash," said Emerald Flower. "The family was ruined in three days. It came about the year before last. The Yellow River had been flooding every other year, and Provincial Governor Zhang was ever so worried about it. It seems there was some high official who was a famous scholar in south China, who showed some book to the governor and said, 'The trouble with this river is that it is too narrow. You will not have peace until it is made broader. You must pull down the people's dikes and keep to the main dikes.' Thereupon all the high officials approved, but the governor said, 'How about the people between the dikes? We shall have to pay them to move their homes.' But those cursed high officials said, 'You must not let the people know. Consider, the distance between the dikes is some two miles broad and two hundred miles long, and thousands of families live there. If you let them know, those hundreds of thousands of men will defend their dikes and make it impossible to pull them down.' The governor could do nothing, so he nodded his head and sighed, and we heard that he even shed a few tears.

"That spring they speedily repaired the main dike and built a secondary dike on the south bank in the district of Jiyang, and those two dikes were the weapon to kill those hundreds of thousands of people; but the poor people did not know it. Then came the sixth month when the people said, 'The water is rising, the water is rising.' The guards on the dikes were kept busy from morning till night, and the water in the river rose one or two feet every day, until in less than ten days it was little lower than the dike, already some twenty feet above the plain. By the middle of the month the runners on the dikes kept coming and going all the time, and on the third day at noon the camps blew their trumpets, gathered their guards and sent them all to the main dike. At that time some shrewd people said, 'It looks bad. Probably trouble is coming. We had better go back quickly and prepare to move our homes.' But nobody could foresee that that night at midnight there would be a great storm. All they heard was a great roar, and the water of the Yellow River rushed down upon them like a mountain. The people in the villages were mostly sleeping in their homes when with this tremendous roar the water rushed in, and by the time they had woken to fly away, the water was already over their roofs. The night was dark, the wind high, and there was a torrent of rain and flood. What do you think they could do?"

If you want to know what happened afterwards, you must read the next chapter.

Chapter Eleven

IT is said that Emerald Flower went on with her story as follows: "By this time it was nearly dawn. The wind dropped, the rain ceased, the clouds dispersed and the moon came out and shone brightly. The state of the village could not be seen, only by the people's dike there were people clinging to doors, tables, chairs and benches, swept against the dike and clambering up it; while the people who lived on the dike took bamboo poles and hurried to the rescue of those in the water, rescuing quite a number. Those whose lives were thus saved, after the first breath, thought how all their family must be lost and they alone surviving, and all of them lamented bitterly. Children called for their fathers and mothers, wives wept for their husbands and parents mourned for their children, until the whole place resounded with the sound of wailing for nearly two hundred miles. You can imagine how pitiable it was, sir."

Then Emerald Ring took up the story, saying, "On that fifteenth day of the sixth month my mother and I happened to be in our shop at the South Gate when in the middle of the night we heard people calling out, 'The water is coming!' Everybody who heard it hastily got up. That day had been particularly hot, and most people had gone to sleep in the courtyard in their underclothes, only going in when it started to rain. They had just fallen into a doze when they heard the shouting outside, and hurried out to the street to look. The city gate was also opened, and people ran outside. Outside the city there was a small dike used to let water out every year; it was about six feet high, and all those people had gone out to reinforce it. At that time the rain had only just stopped, and it was still dark; but in a little while one could just see the people outside the city rushing back as if their lives depended on it. The district magistrate was actually not in his sedan-chair, but was running into the city with the rest. He got up on the city wall and it was just possible to hear him calling out, 'People outside the city must not move in their things. Tell everybody to come in at once! The city is to be closed immediately! There must be no delay!' We all climbed on to the wall too to look, and saw many people using straw to wrap up mud, ready to seal up the city gate. The district magistrate shouted from the city wall, 'Everybody is in now! Close the gates immediately!' Bundles of mud had already been prepared by the citadel, and after closing the gates they sealed them up. I had an uncle called Ji who lived outside the city, and he was up on the wall too.

"After a little while the clouds sank to the mountains and the moon shone very bright. My mother saw Uncle Ji and asked him, 'How is it so bad this year?'

" 'Isn't it terrible?' said Uncle Ji. 'In past years when the flood came, at the start it was only about a foot high, and at the most some two feet high, never exceeding three feet; while by the time it takes to eat one meal the worst flood would have passed, so that it was about two feet on an average. This year the flood is terrible; at the start it was more than a foot, and almost at once it rose to over two feet. The magistrate seeing that it looks bad, and fearing that the small dike will not stand against it, has told people to come into the city at once, for when he gave that order the water had already reached nearly four feet. I haven't seen Brother for the last few days. Was he in the village? I feel rather worried.'

"Then my mother cried, saying, 'That's just it.'

"Suddenly we heard the people on the city wall shouting, 'The water has passed the small dike!' Then everybody rushed down from the wall. My mother sat sobbing on the ground, and said, 'I shall die here. I don't want to go home.' I could do nothing but cry by her side, and I heard people saying, 'Water is leaking through the wall.' Then innumerable people rushed past again; they had no respect for either private houses or shops, but snatched up whatever bedding or clothes they could, taking them to stop up the leaks in the city gate. Very soon they had taken all the clothes from the tailors on the street, and all the cloth from the cloth shops to stop up the cracks in the city wall; and then I heard them say, 'It's not leaking now.' Again I heard, 'The bundles of mud are probably too few to keep the water out.' Thereupon a crowd of people ran to our shop to seize the rice bags to stuff against the leaks in the wall. Soon all the rice was moved away, and they also carried away all the paper from the paper shops and all the cotton from the cotton shops.

"By then it was already dawn, and my mother was dazed with crying. I could do nothing but sit on the ground and keep her company, and I kept hearing people say, 'This flood is really fearful. It must be more than ten feet high. No one ever heard of such a flood before.' Then some of our shop assistants came and carried my mother and myself back; but when we reached the shop we were met by a sorry sight, and the assistants told us, 'Sacks of rice from our shop were used to barricade the city wall, and the loose grain in our granary was all taken by lawless people. Only what was left on the ground we swept together, amounting to some thirty bushels.' There were two women servants in our shop whose homes were in the country, and when they heard of the great flood and knew that their families must have perished, they wept as if they no longer cared to live.

"This went on till the sun was high when the people in our shop succeeded in reviving my mother, and we all had some millet porridge. My mother, when she came to her senses, opened her eyes and asked, 'Where is Grandmother?'

" 'She is sleeping in her room,' they said, 'so we did not like to disturb her.'

" 'We shall have to ask her to get up to eat something,' said Mother. But when she went to her room she found Grandmother was not sleeping, but had died of fright; for when she felt her nostrils there was no breath. When my mother saw this, the porridge she had eaten was thrown up with blood, and she fainted once more; but luckily we had an old maid-servant called Wang, who felt all over the old lady's body, and suddenly cried out, 'It's all right! Her heart is still warm.' Thereupon they tried some artificial respiration, and called for some ginger soup. In the afternoon both my grandmother and my mother recovered consciousness, so the whole family was safe.

"Two of our shop assistants were sitting in the front

court talking. 'They say that the water outside the city wall has reached a height of some fifteen feet,' said one. 'This old city wall may not stand long, and once the water comes in there will not be a single person left alive.'

" 'The magistrate has not yet left the city, so it must be all right,' said the other."

"I heard of this flood too," said Lao Can to Mr. Huang. "Who was responsible for it, and what book did he take as authority, do you know?"

"Since I came the year after the flood I only know of it by hearsay, and I can't say whether what I heard was correct or not," said Mr. Huang. "People said it was the idea of Inspector Shi Junpu, and the book he quoted as authority was the memoranda on river conservancy by Jia Rang of the Han dynasty. 'According to the memoranda,' he said, 'in ancient times the kingdoms of Zhao and Wei had the Yellow River as their common boundary. The kingdoms of Zhao and Wei lay in mountainous regions, while the kingdom of Qi was low-lying; so Qi built a dike eight miles from the river. Then the river on the east side rose to reach the land of Qi, and on the west side flooded the lands of Zhao and Wei, so the kingdoms of Zhao and Wei also constructed dikes eight miles from the river.'

"All the officials were present that day when the inspector pointed out these lines to them, saying, 'This shows the distance between the two dikes was some sixteen miles in the age of the Warring States; thus they had no trouble with the Yellow River. Now the distance between the two dikes is little more than a mile, and even the distance between the main dikes is only about six miles, less than half the distance under the ancient system. Thus unless the people's dikes are pulled down, the river will cause unceasing calamity.'

" 'I understand this reasoning,' said the governor, 'but between the dikes there are villages and farms. If we were to carry out your proposal, would we not destroy tens of thousands of families?'

"But then Inspector Shi showed the memoranda to the governor again, saying, 'Please read what it says here: "People opposing this may declare that this scheme will destroy men's buildings, farms, houses and tombs by tens of thousands, causing the people to murmur. But I say, when Yu pacified the flood he destroyed the mountains which stood in his path. Thus he even destroyed the work of Nature, and this is after all only the handiwork of men." If you are too tender-hearted over small matters, you will jeopardise affairs of great moment. Your Excellency may pity the homes of the people between the dikes, but does not the flood work great havoc every year? This is a project which will ensure eternal peace; thus Jia Rang said in his memoranda, "Our great Han empire has thousands of miles of territory; why should we contend for a few feet of ground with the river?" Once this work is achieved the river will be pacified and the people will rest in peace for thousands of years. Thus it is an excellent plan. Moreover, in the Han dynasty Chinese territory was only some thousands of miles in extent; yet they would not contend with the river. Now the territory of our empire is much greater, and if we contend with the river for land, shall we not cause former sages to laugh at posterity.'

"Then he went on to quote other criticisms of the memoranda saying, 'These three memoranda have become immortal classics; but since the Han dynasty those in charge of river conservancy have all adopted inferior plans, alas! Throughout past dynasties all scholars knew that the three memoranda of Jia Rang were classics, but unfortunately the men responsible for river conservancy were not scholars, and thus the great deed could not be achieved again. If Your Excellency adopts this plan Jia Rang will be grateful to you as his successor after two thousand years, and your achievements will be recorded in history, winning you immortal fame for thousands of generations.'

"Still the governor wrinkled his brow and said, 'I have only one objection: I cannot afford to sacrifice these hundreds of thousands of people.'

"'If this will ensure eternal peace,' said some official, 'why should we not raise some money and move the people away?'

"'That would be the only thing to do,' said the governor. Later I heard they raised some three hundred thousand taels of silver, preparing to move people. Why they did not move them after all I could not say."

Then Mr. Huang said to Emerald Ring, "What happened to you after that? Go on with your story."

"Later my mother decided to leave all to fate," said Emerald Ring, "and if the flood came we must perish."

"I was in Qidong District too that year," said Emerald Flower. "I was staying at the North Gate, because my aunt lived there near the people's dike. There were good shops outside the North Gate and the two small dikes beyond the street were of considerable size, reputed to be thirteen feet high. The ground there was high too, so the water did not reach the North Gate. On the sixteenth of that month I went to the city wall and saw ever so many things floating in the river. There were chests, tables, chairs, benches, windows and doors, to say nothing of the dead people floating everywhere, scattered here and there, and with nobody having time to take up the corpses. The wealthy families were planning to move away, but they could not hire boats."

"Where were the boats?" asked Lao Can.

"They were all commandeered for distributing bread to the people," she said.

"Distributing bread to whom?" he asked. "Why did they need so many boats?"

"That was really a good deed," said Emerald Flower. "Of the people in the villages, more than half were swept away by the flood, while those who survived were the clever ones who climbed on to their roof-tops when the flood came. So in every village there were hundreds of people on the roof-tops; but they were surrounded by water, so how could they get food? Some of them were so hungry that they committed suicide by jumping into the water. Fortunately there were commissioners sent by the governor to distribute bread everywhere in boats, three pieces for each grown-up and two pieces for each child. The next day the commissioners came with empty boats and carried the people to the north bank. Wasn't that a good deed? However there were many fools who stayed on the roofs and would not come down, and when they were asked why, they said that in the water the governor would send them bread, but if they went to the north bank nobody would provide for them and they would die of hunger. Actually the governor only distributed bread for a few days and then stopped; so those people were starved to death. Weren't they fools?"

"This is really fantastic," said Lao Can to Mr. Huang. "Whether it was Inspector Shi's idea or not, the man who introduced this scheme did not have any evil intention, nor did he act from any selfish motives; but because he could only read books and had no practical experience, every step he made was false. Thus Mencius said, 'It is better not to believe in books at all, rather than to believe in them implicitly,' and this is true not only regarding river conservancy. Of all great disasters, only some thirty per cent have been owing to treachery, some seventy per cent being due to inexperienced scholars." Then he asked Emerald Ring, "Did you find your father afterwards, or was he swept away by the flood?"

Emerald Ring wiped her eyes and said, "He must have been swept away by the flood. If he were alive, wouldn't he have gone home?" Then they all sighed.

Lao Can then asked Emerald Flower, "Just now you said that next year she would not even have such a good time as she is having now. What did you mean by that?"

"Our mistress' husband died recently," said Emerald Flower, "and for his funeral more than a hundred strings of cash were spent. Then the other day our mistress gambled at dice and lost two or three hundred strings of cash, making her altogether over four hundred strings short, so that this year she can't possibly manage. So the other day she made up her mind to sell Emerald Ring to Kuai the Baldhead. This Baldhead is notoriously cruel, so that if there is one day when you don't have a client, she takes heated tongs to brand

you. Our mistress wants three hundred taels of silver
from her, but she will only give six hundred strings of
cash, so they have not yet come to an agreement. Just
think, how many days are there left till New Year?
The time is drawing nearer and nearer. By New Year
she will certainly have to sell her, and once Emerald
Ring is sold, don't you suppose she will have all she
can bear?" Lao Can heard but made no comment, while
Emerald Ring wiped away her tears.

"Mr. Tie," said Huang Renrui, "when I said just
now that I wanted to discuss their affairs with you, it
was just on account of this. I think to see an honest
child condemned to such a hell is really a pity. I have
reckoned that this is a matter of not more than three
hundred taels of silver, and I am willing to put up half
that amount if I can find friends to make up the other
half. Won't you contribute a few taels, just as much as
you like? Only I can't give my name as the purchaser
of the girl. If you could take her back with you, this
matter could be very simply arranged. What do you
say?"

"There is nothing difficult about this," said Lao Can.
"As for the silver, if you put up half, I will put up the
other half; for to ask other people for contributions
might not be wise. Only it is out of the question for
me to take her, and you will have to think of some
other arrangement."

When Emerald Ring heard this she hastily knelt down
before the bed and kowtowed to Mr. Huang and Lao
Can, saying, "My two benefactors and saviours, who
are willing to give silver to rescue me from my torment,
I don't care what work you give me as slave-girl or
servant, I shall be grateful for it. Only there is one

thing I should tell you: when I was beaten so often in the past, it was not altogether my mistress who was to blame, but was really my own fault. It was because my mother was starving that she sold me to begin with to this mistress for twenty-four strings of cash, out of which she had to pay three or four strings to the intermediary, only leaving twenty strings. Then last spring my grandmother died, and all the rest of the money was used up. My mother led my younger brother to beg for food, but in half a year, through hunger and privation, she died too. Then only my younger brother was left, who is six years old this year, and it fell to a certain former neighbour of ours, a Mr. Li who also lives in this Qihe District and has a small business, to take him away and give him some scraps to eat from time to time.

"Only that Mr. Li doesn't even have enough for himself, so how can he feed him properly, much less look after his clothing? So when I was in Seven Mile Fair and kind clients happened to give me a string of cash, every two months I saved up two or three strings of cash, and sent them to him. Now that you kind gentlemen have saved me, if you send me within a distance of a hundred miles that won't matter, for I shall be able to save a little money to send him; but if I am sent far away I beg you two gentlemen to think of a way so that I can take the child with me, or put him in a temple or find a small family to look after him. Then our Tian family ancestral ghosts for the last hundred generations will be grateful to you, and will certainly reward you. Alas, our poor Tian family now depends on this one slender branch." When she had spoken she burst into tears again, while Mr. Huang said, "This is not too easy."

"What is difficult about that?" asked Lao Can. "I can think of a way myself." Then he called out, "Miss Tian, there is no need for you to cry! I will guarantee that you and your young brother need not be separated as long as you live. Don't cry! Let us think out a good plan for you. If you confuse us by your crying we can't think of a good plan. Quickly stop crying." Hearing this Emerald Ring at once restrained her tears and knocked her head on the ground before them with resounding thumps. Lao Can hastily raised her up, but she had already knocked her head so violently that her forehead was bruised and bleeding. He quickly made her sit down, and said, "Why should you do that?" And having wiped the blood gently from her forehead, he made her lie down on the bed.

Then Lao Can turned to discuss the question with Mr. Huang, saying, "Regarding the management of this affair, we must work out the different stages. To ransom her is the first stage, and to find her a suitable husband is the second. Regarding the ransom, it is divided again into stages; in the first stage we will try private negotiation, and if that fails we will take the case to court. At present other people have offered six hundred strings, so tomorrow we shall call the mistress here and offer her six hundred strings also, then gradually increase the amount. It doesn't do to be too generous with such people, for if we are too generous she will feel that she has great bargaining power. At this moment the silver exchange is one tael to two strings and seven hundred cash, so three hundred taels can be exchanged for eight hundred strings. This will certainly be enough, including incidental expenditures. Let us wait and see the attitude of the mistress. If she is not obstinate, private negotiation is best; but if she is suspicious and difficult, we will ask the district magistrate to decide the matter for us at court; then we shall again conclude the bargain privately. What do you think?"

"Very good, very good," said Mr. Huang.

"Of course," went on Lao Can, "you cannot let your name come into this, and I don't want my name to appear either; so we will say that we are doing it for a relative of ours. When the affair is settled then we will make it clear that we are going to choose her a husband, for otherwise her mistress will not let her go."

"Very good," said Mr. Huang. "An excellent plan."

"Regarding silver, we shall pay fifty-fifty, no matter how much it is; but what I have with me on my travels is not enough, so you will have to advance the money for me, and as soon as I return to the provincial capital I shall repay you."

"That's all right," said Mr. Huang. "I have more money than necessary for ransoming two Emerald Rings. Provided the matter is satisfactorily settled it doesn't matter whether you pay me back or not."

"Of course I shall pay you back," said Lao Can. "I have more than four hundred taels of silver in the bank, so you needn't be afraid that I may not be able to pay, or that I shan't have enough left for my livelihood. You may rest assured."

"Then that is settled," said Mr. Huang. "Tomorrow morning I will tell people to summon the mistress."

"Don't call for her tomorrow morning," said Emerald Flower, "for we have to go back tomorrow morning, and if you call for her then and she knows your intention, she will hide Emerald Ring in the country before dicussing business; then you will have to do as she wants. Besides, these opium smokers do not get up early. The best thing would be tomorrow afternoon, having first told people to fetch us here, you summon our mistress; for then we shall have nothing to fear from her. Only one thing: don't say that I told you this. Emerald Ring is the lucky one who need not fear the mistress any more; but I have still some years to live in this hell."

"Of course," said Mr. Huang. "That goes without saying. Tomorrow I will go first to the office and bring back a bailiff. If your mistress is difficult, then I will entrust Emerald Ring to the bailiff, and we shall have her at our mercy." After this decision they all felt very pleased; but if you want to know what happened afterwards, you must read the next chapter.

Chapter Twelve

IT is said that no sooner had Lao Can and Mr. Huang decided upon their plan for rescuing Emerald Ring, and just as they stopped speaking, Emerald Ring raised her head and cried out, "Look how red the window is!" She had barely finished speaking when they heard a great crash and the sound of many voices outside, all shouting, "Fire! Fire!" They hastily ran out of the room, and when they raised the door-screen they saw that the fire was raging at the back of Lao Can's chamber. Lao Can hastily took out his key and unlocked the door, while Mr. Huang called out, "Some people come! Help Mr. Tie to move his things out." But when Lao Can unlocked his door and pushed it open, a great cloud of black smoke belched out, and the fire began to spread through the window. At the great belch of smoke Lao Can hastily retreated; but he tripped over a brick and fell down. Just then, however, some men arrived to move away his things, and helping Lao Can up they assisted him to the east side of the building.

When they looked at the fire it seemed as if it would spread to the other rooms too, so Mr. Huang's servant, leading the others, went to his master's rooms to carry out his things. Mr. Huang standing in the courtyard called out, "Quickly bring out that case of mine. Other things can wait." By this time however his servant had already moved out the case while the others carried out the rest of Mr. Huang's baggage, putting it at the foot of the eastern wall. The hotel manager had meanwhile sent over several long benches for them to sit down on, and Mr. Huang looking through his possessions found that not only was there nothing missing but there was even one additional piece; so he hastily ordered the servants to move these things to the hotel storeroom. Gentle reader, can you guess what that additional piece was? It was Emerald Flower's bedding. Mr. Huang knew that the magistrate would be coming to inspect the fire, and if he should see this it would be rather embarrassing, so he ordered the servants to move the things away, and said to the two girls, "You two had better hide in the store-room too. The magistrate will be here presently." When the two girls heard this they walked away skirting the wall.

It is said that when the fire started all the neighbours, to say nothing of the boatmen and servants, brought barrels and basins to extinguish it. However, as the two banks of the Yellow River were frozen, although there was some flowing water in the middle, people could not reach it, and the big pool behind the hotel was frozen too. Outside the city there were only two wells with water, but if they carried this water slowly, barrel by barrel, it would not serve any purpose. However in the emergency they hit upon a plan: they broke the ice in the pool and threw it into the fire piece by piece, and the ice actually proved more efficacious than water; for wherever a piece of ice was thrown, the flames would die down. The pool was just behind Mr. Huang's rooms and some seven or eight men stood on the roof, while behind them several dozen people carried ice on to the roof, which they took over and threw into the flames.

Half the ice fell into the fire and half over the rooms, so that the conflagration was unable to spread to Mr. Huang's quarters.

Lao Can and Mr. Huang were by the eastern wall watching people putting out the fire, when a procession of lanterns and torches heralded the arrival of the magistrate. He led in his men, all carrying long poles with hooks to help put out the fire; but when they entered the gate the fire was already nearly extinguished. Some of them pulled down debris with their hooks, some of them went to fetch thin pieces of ice from the river to throw into the flames to keep them down, and thus the fire was eventually extinguished.

The magistrate then caught sight of Mr. Huang standing under the eastern wall, and came over to greet him, saying, "You must have been rather alarmed, sir."

"I am all right," said Mr. Huang, "only my friend has suffered considerably." Then he said to the magistrate, "Mr. Wang, let me introduce a friend. His name is Tie Bucan."

"Oh, is Mr. Tie here?" said the magistrate. "I would like to meet him."

Mr. Huang then waved to him and shouted, "Mr. Tie, come over here."

Lao Can had been sitting on the same bench as Mr. Huang, but when the magistrate came towards them he had joined the crowd, pretending to watch the fire; now that Mr. Huang called him he went over, greeted the magistrate and said a few polite words. The magistrate had his own stool so Lao Can and Mr. Huang still sat on the long bench. This magistrate was called Wang Zijin, and he was also from south of the river, and a native of Lao Can's district. Although he was a government scholar he was no fool. By this time the fire was completely burnt out, and the magistrate wanted to take them to spend the night in the yamen, but Mr. Huang said, "Since my room has escaped burning, I can still move back; but Mr. Tie has now no home to return to."

"That doesn't matter," said Lao Can. "The night is already nearly spent, and it will soon be dawn; then I shall go to the street to buy bedding. It won't be inconvenient." When the magistrate insisted that Lao Can should go to the yamen, the latter said, "I don't mind troubling Mr. Huang, so don't worry about me."

Then the magistrate, looking much concerned, asked, "What did you lose in the fire? You must have lost much that was of great value. But whatever we can procure in our district, we shall try to make good your loss to the best of our ability."

Lao Can laughed and replied, "One set of bedding, one bamboo case, two pairs of cotton underwear, some old books and one iron clapper: that's all." The magistrate smiled and said, "That couldn't be all," and they all laughed.

Just as the magistrate was about to leave, the local headman and bailiff led in a man in chains, who knelt on the ground kowtowing continuously like a chicken pecking rice, and crying without stop, "May Your Grace have mercy! May Your Grace have mercy!" The headman knelt on one knee and reported, "The fire started in this old man's room. May I ask Your Grace whether we should take him to the yamen or investigate the case here?"

The magistrate then questioned the man: "What is

your name and from what district are you? How did the fire start?"

The prisoner, kneeling, kowtowed again and said, "My name is Zhang, of this district, working as a servant in the neighbouring hotel. Yesterday I was busy from daybreak till nearly midnight before I was free to go back to my room to sleep; but my underclothes were soaked with sweat and lying down I felt very cold and could not stop shivering, so that I could not go to sleep. I saw there was a lot of straw in the room, so I took some and burnt it to warm myself; then I remembered there was wine left by the visitors for me by the window-ledge, so I warmed it by the fire and drank a few cups. But as I was tired out, what with the warmth and some cups of wine inside me, somehow as I was sitting there I fell asleep. I had just dropped off when in a very short time I was conscious of smoke choking me. I opened my eyes at once and saw my padded coat was already partly burnt, while the matting wall had caught fire; so I quickly ran out to look for water, but by then the fire had spread through the roof and I could do nothing. This is the whole truth. May Your Grace have mercy!"

"Fool!" exclaimed the magistrate. "Take him to the yamen." Then he stood up, and saying good-bye to Mr. Huang and Lao Can he hurriedly departed.

The fire was now completely extinguished, and there was only white smoke to be seen. Mr. Huang saw his servant direct men to carry his things back to his rooms and put them in order, and said, "There is still a smell of smoke about the rooms. Better burn some incense to drive the smell away." Then he smiled and said to

Lao Can, "Now do you still insist on going back to your room?"

"This was all because you insisted on keeping me," said Lao Can. "If I had been in my room, my things would not all have been lost."

"Is that so?" said Mr. Huang. "If I had let you go, you would probably have been burnt alive. You are really an ungrateful wretch to complain instead of thanking me."

"Do you take me for a dead man incapable of movement?" asked Lao Can. "If you don't make good my loss, you needn't think I shall let you off."

As they were speaking the door-screen was raised and Mr. Huang's servant ushered in a bailiff wearing a tall hat, who bowed to Lao Can and said, "My master's compliments, and we have brought some bedding. It is our master's own, and he hopes, sir, you will excuse its being slightly soiled. Tomorrow we shall lose no time in calling the tailor to make new bedding and bring it over. Our master hopes you can put up with this for the night. There is also a fox-skin coat and jacket which he hopes you will accept."

Lao Can stood up and said, "I am sorry to have troubled your master. I shall keep the bedding here for the time being and borrow it for a few days until I have bought some for myself, when I shall return it. As for clothes, all that I had I am wearing, and they were not burnt; so I shall not trouble your master for any. Please thank your master for me when you go back."

But the bailiff would not take back the clothes until Mr. Huang said to him, "Mr. Tie will certainly not accept the clothes. You can tell your master that I told you to take them back." Then the bailiff bowed again and went out.

"It doesn't matter that my things were burnt," said Lao Can, "but it was due entirely to your trouble-making that Emerald Ring's bedding was burnt as well. Can you deny that that might have been avoided?"

"That matters even less," said Mr. Huang. "Regarding her bedding, it can't be worth ten taels of silver altogether. Tomorrow I will give her fifteen taels and her mistress will not be able to contain herself for joy."

"Yes, indeed," said Emerald Ring. "It must be owing to my bad luck that this bedding and so many good things of Mr. Tie's were lost."

"I had nothing valuable except two Song-dynasty editions, which can't be bought with money," said Lao Can, "and that is a pity. But this seems to be fate, so we must submit to it."

"I don't think Song-dynasty editions matter," said Mr. Huang. "The only pity is that your physician's clapper is destroyed, for that means you will lose your livelihood."

"Yes. You will have to pay for that at least," said Lao Can. "You can't refuse to do that."

Mr. Huang then stood up and said to him, "All right, all right. Her bedding is burnt and your clapper is burnt. This is most auspicious. Congratulations." So he bowed to Emerald Ring and to Lao Can, saying, "From now on she will not have to sell herself and you won't have to act as a quack."

"Very good," shouted Lao Can. "Nicely cursed! Emerald Ring, why don't you go and pinch his lips?"

"Amida Buddha!" said Emerald Ring. "You are both very kind."

Then Emerald Flower nodded and said, "Emerald Ring will henceforward lead a good life, and Mr. Tie will in future become an official; so this fire is a very auspicious fire. I must congratulate you both also."

"If what you say is true," said Lao Can, "she will be leading a good life, but I shall be leading a bad one."

They warmed themselves over the brazier, chatting casually, and so two or three hours slipped away without their noticing it, until the east was already beginning to grow bright, and Mr. Huang said, "Now we should have some sleep." So Mr. Huang and Lao Can lay down on the two ends of the bed, while the two girls lay down in the middle, and very soon they were all sound asleep.

When they woke up it was already noon, and the man from the girls' mistress was waiting to take them back. He rolled up the bedding to take it away, and Mr. Huang said, "Bring them back this evening. We shall not send anyone to fetch them." The man assented and went out with the two girls, while Emerald Ring turned her head, her eyes filled with tears, saying, "Don't forget." Mr. Huang and Lao Can nodded smiling. Then they washed their faces, rested for a while and had lunch. By the time they had finished lunch it was after two o'clock, and Mr. Huang went to the yamen. He returned after two hours, saying, "The magistrate wanted to invite you there to dinner; but I said, 'That's not good; it would be better to send over a good feast and let me act as host for you.' So I am entrusted with this task. What do you think of it?"

"Fine," said Lao Can. "You have a free meal, while I am put under an obligation to him. That is all very well for you, but what will you eat if I send the feast back?"

"If you think you can send it back," said Mr. Huang, "then do as you please. I shall starve together with you."

As they were speaking a man wearing a cap with red tassels came to the door holding a visiting card, followed by a man carrying a hamper. He came to the room, lifted the screen and entered, and asked Mr. Huang, glancing towards Lao Can, "Is this Mr. Tie?"

"Yes," said Mr. Huang.

Then the messenger went forward and saluted Lao Can, saying, "Our master says this is a poor district and we have nothing good to eat; so he has sent over a simple meal, and hopes you will put up with it, sir."

"Meals are very convenient here," said Lao Can, "so that your master need not trouble. Please take it back and send it to someone else."

"My master ordered me to beg you to accept it," said the messenger, "and I dare not take it back or I shall be reprimanded."

Mr. Huang meanwhile had taken a piece of paper from the table, and a brush, and now he said to the servant, "Tell them to carry it to the kitchen." The messenger opened the hamper for their inspection, and it was a very sumptuous feast with shark's fins; so Lao Can said, "We should not even accept a simple meal, but this is much too lavish. We cannot take it." However Mr. Huang had already written a note which he handed to the messenger, saying, "This is Mr. Tie's reply. Take it back and thank your master for us." Then he told his man to give the messenger a string of cash and two hundred cash to the man carrying the hamper.

The messenger saluted them both, thanked them and left.

Then Mr. Huang's servant brought in the lamp, and in less than half an hour the two girls arrived, and the man accompanying them without waiting for orders carried their bedding into the room.

"Your bedding was made very quickly," said Mr. Huang, "to be ready in half a day."

"There is plenty of bedding in our place," said Emerald Flower. "We have more than enough."

The servant came in and asked, "Are you ready for dinner, sir?" And Mr. Huang replied that they were. After a little while the dishes were ready, and Mr. Huang said, "Although the north wind has dropped today, it is still very cold. Let us quickly warm some wine and drink a few cups; and since today we are particularly happy, let us drink a little more." The two girls took their guitars and sang a couple of songs to accompany the drinking, until Mr. Huang said, "No need to sing. Come and drink with us."

When Emerald Ring heard this she suddenly frowned and became silent. This was because she thought that although they were powerful it was impossible to tell whether they had meant what they said the night before or not; and if they had spoken casually, once this opportunity was lost she would never have such a chance again all her life. So she frowned. Then she thought again how her mistress would certainly have her sold by the end of the year, and Kuai the Baldhead was so fierce that sooner or later she would surely die; and at that her face became ashen pale. Again she thought how she was a girl from a respectable family, now sunk so low that it was really better to die, and her face took on a resolute expression. But yet, she reasoned, if she died, although she would have nothing to regret, there would be no one to look after her six-year-old brother, so that he would surely die of starvation too; and if he were to die of starvation not only would there be no one to do sacrifice to her parents' ghosts, but it would mean the end of the family; therefore she knew she could not die. So, thinking this way and that, she felt she could neither live nor die; thus she could not prevent her tears from falling, and hastily took her handkerchief to wipe them away.

Emerald Flower seeing this said, "You silly girl. The gentlemen are happy today. What has possessed you again?"

Mr. Huang looking at her only smiled, while Lao Can nodded to her and said, "Don't go imagining things. We will think out a way to help you."

"All right," said Mr. Huang. "With Mr. Tie helping you, what I said last night need not be counted."

Hearing this Emerald Ring felt even more sure that what she feared was true. She was just going to question Mr. Huang when the servant led in a messenger who saluted Mr. Huang and handed him a red envelope. Mr. Huang took the envelope, opened it and looked inside, put it in his pocket, saying, "I understand." After which he laughed incessantly to himself. Then the servant asked, "Would you come out for a few minutes, sir?" And Mr. Huang went out and was absent for half an hour before he walked slowly back and found the three others silent there without a word, and this only seemed to increase his delight.

Then the magistrate's servant came in and saluted

Lao Can, saying, "My master told me to take back the bedding sent yesterday."

"What is this?" thought Lao Can in surprise. "If he takes that away what shall I use tonight?" But since the bedding was not his he could not insist on keeping it, so he said, "Very well, take it away." But he felt somewhat taken aback. He saw the servant go to his room and take the bedding out, and then Mr. Huang said, "Today we were very happy, but since Emerald Ring is sad I am not happy any more. I won't drink any more wine. Take the dishes away." Then the servant came in and did indeed take away the dishes, whereat not only were the two girls surprised, but even Lao Can felt bewildered. After this the servant brought in the man from the procuress, who took Emerald Ring's bedding away also.

"But why, why?" asked Emerald Ring hastily. "Don't they want me here?"

"I don't know," said the man. "I only have orders to take the bedding back."

Emerald Ring could now no longer contain herself, and was convinced that some disaster was impending; so with tears in her eyes she knelt down before Mr. Huang and said, "Although I am worthless, won't you gentlemen be merciful? Once you are angry we shall die."

"I am perfectly happy," said Mr. Huang. "Why shouldn't I be? But regarding your affair, it is not my business. You go and speak to Mr. Tie."

Emerald Ring then knelt to Lao Can, and said, "You, sir, must save me."

"Why?" said Lao Can. "Why should I save you?"

"Now they are taking away the bedding," said Emerald Ring, "it must mean that last night's conversation is known to our mistress, and she will not let me stay here today but is going to force me back so that tomorrow she can take me far away. For what chance has she against officials? Flight is the best policy for her."

"What she says is right," said Lao Can. "We must find a way to help her. Once her mistress takes her back, it is going to be difficult."

"Of course, you should keep her," said Mr. Huang. "But if you don't keep her who else can?"

Lao Can helped Emerald Ring up, at the same time saying to Mr. Huang, "I don't understand you. Do you really mean that what you said last night goes for nothing?"

"I have thought it over thoroughly," said Mr. Huang, "and I can have nothing to do with it. Just think for yourself. To ransom a girl one must have a pretext; but if you don't want to be involved, and I don't want to be involved, then what can we do? Even if we do take her out, where should we put her? If we have her in the hotel while neither of us will have her as his concubine, outsiders will certainly think me responsible; but I have just been promoted and there are many people jealous of me who would certainly tell the governor; in which case I should not be able to work any longer in Shandong, much less think of promotion. Thus I must definitely be out of it."

Upon reflection Lao Can knew that his argument was sound; but still he could not endure the thought of not rescuing a girl from shame because of this, so he said again to Mr. Huang, "Even so we must think of some good plan."

"You think," said Mr. Huang. "If you hit upon a plan I will certainly help."

Lao Can racked his brains but could not think of a plan, so he said, "Although there seems to be no way, we must reconsider it carefully."

"I have a plan," said Mr. Huang, "only you would not agree to it, so there is no need to mention it."

"Just say what it is," said Lao Can, "and I will try to do it."

"You must agree to have her as your concubine; then we shall have a pretext."

"All right," said Lao Can.

"Do you think a casual promise is enough?" said Mr. Huang. "I am taking charge of this, and if I tell people that you want her for your concubine, who would believe me? I can only do it if you write me a letter in your own handwriting."

"That's difficult to write," said Lao Can.

"I knew you wouldn't do it," said Mr. Huang.

Lao Can was hesitating when the two girls pleaded to him together, saying, "What does it matter to you? Do consent, sir."

"How shall I write this letter?" asked Lao Can.

"Naturally you will write to the magistrate," said Mr. Huang. "You can say, 'So-and-so, a singing girl, originally belonged to a good family, but is now in a pitiable condition, and I want to take her out of this bad society and make her my concubine. Please condescend to help me. I shall return you the ransom money later.' With such a letter I shall be able to do it, and afterwards you will be free either to present her to someone else or to choose a husband for her, and I shall escape slander. Otherwise how can it be done?"

Just as he was speaking, the servant came in and said, "Mistress Emerald Ring, people from your mistress are asking for you." When Emerald Ring heard this, her soul seemed to take flight and she wrinkled her brow, at the same time begging Lao Can to write the letter. Emerald Flower simultaneously took out paper, brush and ink from the inner room, wet the brush and gave it to Lao Can, who sighed and said to Emerald Ring, "It seems it can't be helped. For your sake I shall have to put my name to a statement."

"I will kowtow to you a thousand times," said Emerald Ring. "This that you are doing is better than building a seven-storied pagoda."

By then Lao Can had finished writing, and he gave the letter to Mr. Huang, saying, "My work is done. If you still can't arrange it satisfactorily that will be your fault." Mr. Huang took the letter, gave it to his servant, and said, "Take this to the yamen presently."

During the time that Lao Can was writing his letter, Mr. Huang had whispered many words into Emerald Flower's ear, and when the servant took the letter he said to Emerald Ring, "Your mistress is waiting for you. Better go quickly." But still Emerald Ring would not go, looking at Mr. Huang, mutely imploring his help. "Never mind," said Mr. Huang. "You can go. I will look after everything." Thereupon Emerald Flower stood up, and taking Emerald Ring's hand, said, "If I go with you, will you worry? There is really nothing at all to worry about." Then Emerald Ring could do nothing, so she said, "Excuse me," and went out.

Mr. Huang then lay down on the bed to smoke, and talked casually with Lao Can. After about an hour, when Mr. Huang had finished smoking, his servant came in wearing a brand-new tall hat, and said, "Please come over, sir."

"Oh!" said Mr. Huang; then standing up he drew Lao Can with him saying, "Let's sit over there."

Lao Can was surprised and said, 'Where is this 'over there'?"

"This 'over there' came into being today," said Mr. Huang. For the inner chambers of the hotel consisted of two suites, each with three rooms. Mr. Huang occupied the three rooms on the west and there were also three rooms on the east which had previously been occupied; but that morning the former occupant had left to cross the river, leaving the rooms vacant. The two men went hand in hand to the rooms on the east side, and by the time they climbed the steps someone had already lifted the screen. Above the square table in the middle hung a canopy, on the table were two red candles and on the floor a red rug. When they entered the hall they noticed that in the room on the east side there was another square table facing south, also with a canopy, while on the north side there were two chairs side by side with two other chairs one on each side, all with cushions. The table was covered with candied fruit, looking even more tempting than that offered to them before; and the room on the west side had a red velvet door-screen.

"What is this?" Lao Can was beginning to ask in surprise when he heard Mr. Huang call out, "Bring the young lady out to see her master." Then the screen was lifted and a maid-servant on the left and Emerald Flower on the right helped out a beautiful girl with flowers covering her head, wearing a purple cloak, green tunic and rose skirt, who walked with lowered head to the red rug. Lao Can looking closely, saw that this was Emerald Ring, and shouted aloud, "What is this? This won't do!"

"You have already signed the statement," said Mr. Huang. "What more have you to say?" And without listening to his protests he dragged Lao Can towards a chair; but he would not sit down. By this time Emerald Ring had already bowed down before him, so Lao Can could not do anything but bow back, and the maid-servant said, "Please sit down, Mr. Huang; the go-between must be thanked." Then Emerald Ring bowed to him also, while Mr. Huang said, "Oh, no, no," and bowed to her in return. Then they took the bride back to her room.

Emerald Flower presently came out and bowed in congratulation, and the maid-servants and others all offered their congratulations too. Mr. Huang took Lao Can to the bridal chamber where the new beddings were all made ready. There were two sets of red and green silk quilts, two red and green velvet rugs, and two pillows. Before the bed there was a purple silk curtain, on the table a red tablecloth and a pair of red candles, and on the wall a pair of red scrolls on which was written:

> "Let us hope that all lovers in the world will be married,
> For when it is predestined one must not lose one's opportunity."

Lao Can recognised Mr. Huang's writing, but the ink was not yet dry, so laughing at him, he said, "You are really a devil. These words are taken from the Marriage God's Temple in the West Lake. You have stolen them."

"The words are good," retorted Mr. Huang, "and can you say that they are not appropriate?" Then he took from his pocket the red envelope sent by the magistrate, and gave it to Lao Can saying, "Look, this is the former sale's receipt of your concubine, and this is the new receipt. I present you with both of them together. Don't you think I am very thorough in the management of business."

"Since this is done I am most grateful," said Lao Can, "but why should you want to involve me in this?"

"Didn't I say that if a thing is predestined one must not lose one's opportunity?" said Mr. Huang. "For Emerald Ring's sake you had to do this, to make her secure; for when I rescue a person I like to do it properly. And from your point of view you don't lose anything either. All affairs should be managed like this." After saying this he laughed heartily and said, "Let's talk no more nonsense. I am ravenous. Let us have dinner now." So he pulled Lao Can, and Emerald Flower pulled Emerald Ring, urging them to sit in the two seats of honour; but Lao Can definitely declined, so finally they took down the canopy and the four sat down facing each other. During the feast it goes without saying that everyone was happy and the feast ended happily. Then the bride and bridegroom were sent to their chamber to sleep: there is no need to go into details.

It is said that since Lao Can was forced into marriage by Mr. Huang, he could not feel satisfied until he had taken his revenge; also he noticed that Emerald Flower had done a great deal for Emerald Ring, and that from an outsider's point of view she was a good-hearted girl, so she deserved to be ransomed too. But he would have to await his opportunity.

The next day Mr. Huang came in and smiled at Emerald Ring, saying, "Did you sleep well by the corner of the bed last night?"

"I owe everything to your great kindness," said Emerald Ring. "In future I shall keep your shrine to worship."

"That would be too much," said Mr. Huang. Then he said to Lao Can, "Yesterday the three hundred taels of silver were paid by the magistrate, so today I am going to the yamen to pay them for you. Those clothes and bedding were also a present from the magistrate; but you need not be polite about them, for if you try to repay him, he will not let you."

"That is too much," said Lao Can, "making other people spend so much on my account. You thank him first for me, and I shall try to repay him later." Mr. Huang then went to the yamen.

Lao Can considered Emerald Ring's name rather vulgar, moreover it would not be convenient to continue to call her by that name; so he inverted the two words, making the new name Ring Emerald, and this used as a pet name sounded better. In the afternoon he sent people to fetch her brother, and when he noticed that his clothes were ragged he gave him a few taels of silver and told that Mr. Li to take him away again to buy some clothes for him. Time passed very quickly, and soon five days had slipped away.

One day when Mr. Huang had gone to the yamen and Lao Can was in the hotel teaching Ring Emerald to read, he suddenly heard the hotel people announcing, "The magistrate is coming." Presently the magistrate's sedan-chair arrived in the courtyard, and he descended from his chair while Lao Can went out of the door to welcome him. The magistrate came in and they sat down, and the magistrate said, "I came here to offer my congratulations and have a chat."

"The other day I was very grateful to you," said Lao Can, "and asked Mr. Huang to express my thanks to you; but I have not yet been myself to thank you. I hope you will excuse me."

"Don't mention it," replied the magistrate. Then Lao Can told his concubine to come out to see him, and the magistrate presented a few trinkets as gifts.

"The other day," said Lao Can, "I asked people to take you three hundred taels of silver to repay you. Did you receive them?"

"Not only did I receive them," replied the magistrate, "but I have received too much. Mr. Huang also sent me three hundred taels, and then you sent me three hundred taels, so that is too much. However I must pay both of you back."

Lao Can reflected for a moment, and said, "Mr. Huang also has a friend whose name is Emerald Flower, who belongs to the same house as my concubine, and is quite a good-natured girl. Since Mr. Huang is also rather lonely away from home, would you not get him a concubine too, using these two sums of money for the purchase?" The magistrate clapped his hands in approval and immediately gave orders to his bailiff, telling him to have this done the next day.

The next day Lao Can went to the yamen and learnt that four hundred and twenty taels of silver had been used to purchase Emerald Flower. The magistrate insisted on repaying him three hundred taels of sil-

ver, but Lao Can would only accept one hundred and
eighty. That night he told the hotel manager to hire a
cart and fetch Ring Emerald's brother. And so he and
Ring Emerald and her brother, together with Mr.
Huang and Emerald Flower left the next day at dawn
to return at last to the provincial capital.

老 残 游 记

刘 鹗

熊 猫 丛 书

＊

《中国文学》杂志社出版
（中国百万庄路24号）
中国国际书店发行
1983年（36开）第1版
编号：（英）2—916—16
00130
10—E—1751